DISCARDED

Columbia University

Contributions to Education

Teachers College Series

No. 250

AMS PRESS
NEW YORK

THE COURTS
AND
THE CURRICULUM

BY

OTTO TEMPLAR HAMILTON, Ph.D.

TEACHERS COLLEGE, COLUMBIA UNIVERSITY
CONTRIBUTIONS TO EDUCATION, No. 250

BUREAU OF PUBLICATIONS
Teachers College, Columbia University
NEW YORK CITY
1927

Library of Congress Cataloging in Publication Data

Hamilton, Otto Templar, 1883-
  The courts and the curriculum.

  Reprint of the 1927 ed., issued in series: Teachers
College, Columbia University. Contributions to
education, no. 250.
  Originally presented as the author's thesis, Columbia.
  Bibliography: p.
  1. Educational law and legislation--United States--
States. 2. Education--United States--States--Curricula.
I. Title. II. Series: Columbia University. Teachers
College. Contributions to education, no. 250.
KF4201.Z95H34 1972   344'.73'077   73-176834
ISBN 0-404-55250-1

Reprinted by Special Arrangement with Teachers
College Press, New York, New York

From the edition of 1927, New York
First AMS edition published in 1972
Manufactured in the United States

AMS PRESS, INC.
NEW YORK, N. Y.   10003

ACKNOWLEDGMENTS

The author welcomes the opportunity of thanking those who have been of special assistance to him in the preparation of this study. An expression of appreciation is due primarily to the chairman of the committee in charge of the study, Professor N. L. Lngelhardt, of Teachers College. He always gave generously of his time and advice in guiding the work. Thanks are particularly due to Professor Frederick C. Hicks, of Columbia University, for his kindly interest in the study, his assistance in making available the legal sources necessary for the investigation, and his very valuable advice in regard to the legal phases of the work. Professors William F. Russell, Adelaide T. Case, and Frederick G. Bonser each gave helpful suggestions. Thanks are also due to Professors George D. Strayer and J. R. McGaughy for their counsel and advice throughout the period of the study. Professors Carter Alexander and Paul R. Mort also gave assistance from time to time. Miss Edna J. Gregg and Miss Lenore Ramsey, teachers in the high school at Fairmount, Indiana, read the manuscript and suggested corrections and improvements.

The author cannot refrain from expressing his appreciation of the inspiration and help that have come to him. at all times from his wife and his mother. Since childhood his mother has constantly encouraged him to undertake further study. Throughout the many months of preparation for the study and the year that has been devoted chiefly to the work, his wife has continually been a source of inspiration and of cheer. To her, more than to any other person, are due the sincere thanks of the author.

CONTENTS

Contents

Contents

THE COURTS
AND
THE CURRICULUM

CHAPTER I

INTRODUCTION

STATEMENT OF THE PROBLEM

The people of the United States have an abiding faith in education. They spend enormous sums for public schools. These schools exist only in order that children may be instructed. Instructed in what? There is at the present time widespread interest in the instruction the public schools are now giving and may give in the future to the children of our land. Curriculum study and research are being carried on in all parts of the United States by the teaching profession. Economic, political, social and religious interests and organizations are studying the curriculum, proposing changes, and attempting in various ways to have their proposals carried into effect.

Regardless of who proposes changes or innovations in the curriculum or why they propose them, people differ as to the advisability of making such changes. These differences lead to controversies and oftentimes these controversies lead to the courts. Many of these controversial curricular problems are carried to the higher judicial tribunals for final adjudication. In this way the courts of our land are called upon to settle issues dealing with the curriculum and thereby exert an important influence upon the curriculum of the public schools. This study deals with the relation of the courts to the curriculum as revealed by the facts of cases and the decisions of judges—particularly in the higher courts.

Do those who are interested in the curriculum of the public schools understand to what extent the attitude of the courts has

1

been responsible for the present scope and content of that curriculum? Do they have in mind the principles that have formed the basis for the decisions which the courts have made upon curricular controversies in the past? Are the tendencies which the courts have shown in their decisions in the past and the principles which they have laid down in deciding curricular controversies recognized by all those persons who propose changes in the curriculum? Is there a general realization of the fact that these tendencies and principles are sure to have a bearing upon the decision of similar controversies in the future?

It is important that all persons who are interested in the harmonious development of the public schools and in the introduction into them of the most satisfactory curriculum and curricular practices that it is possible to evolve should have knowledge concerning these issues. Perhaps the results of this study may tend to reduce the number of controversies arising out of curricular problems and to bring about an easier solution of some of the difficulties of providing a satisfactory curriculum.

PURPOSE OF THE STUDY

This study has been made for the purpose of:

1. Discovering those issues, pertinent to the curriculum of the public common schools, that have been adjudicated by the higher judicial tribunals of the states and the nation.

2. Isolating and revealing some legal principles that have been decisive of cases in which the issues involved were related to the curriculum of the public schools, and which might serve as practical aids to those who may be confronted by legal questions pertaining to the curriculum.

3. Attempting to discover trends in the attitude of the judicial tribunals toward issues pertinent to the curriculum.

SOURCES OF THE DATA

The reports of the cases from the state reporter systems of the various states and the United States reports in the law library of Columbia University were the chief source of the data used in the study. The various sets of annotated reports, the statutes and constitutions of the several states and of the United States, and the decisions of the chief educational officer of New York were also used as a source. In a few instances textbooks and reports of research investigations were used as cited in the body of the study.

THE METHOD OF PROCEDURE

Locating and Selecting the Cases Used. Through the aid of the various digests and search books, available for this specific purpose in the law library, about 800 cases were listed as having possibilities of a bearing upon the curriculum. These cases were then read to determine whether they contained data pertinent to this study. The citations in the cases read added many cases to the list of possibilities. About 600 cases remained after this process of elimination.

Collecting and Organizing the Data. The necessary data were collected from the reports of the cases and placed on 5×8 cards for convenience in filing and classification. Short quotations were placed on the cards. Notations were made as to the desirability and location of longer quotations. About 140 cases of particular importance were more extensively briefed on $8\frac{1}{2} \times 11$ paper and used for quick reference purposes.

The final efforts at classification resulted in about 100 subtopics grouped under the following general headings, which have been used as chapter headings:

1. The Scope of the Curriculum.
2. Control of the Curriculum by Legislative Action.
3. Control of the Curriculum by Local Agencies.
4. Religion and the Bible in the Public Schools.
5. Instructional Supplies.
6. The Adoption and Change of Textbooks.

The chapter headings used are not mutually exclusive in all instances but they seem to be as good as could be obtained. "Instructional Supplies" and "The Adoption and Change of Textbooks" are not as closely related to the curriculum as the other chapter headings but, nevertheless, they do have an important effect upon it.

Reporting the Data. The first draft of the study was made in the law library with the cases at hand for reference and verification. Every reasonable effort has been made to interpret and report the data accurately, but perhaps it is too much to hope that no errors have crept into the study.

Liberal quotations have been made from the decisions. In a limited study like this they could not be given concerning every issue in a case, nor was it possible to include quotations from every decision. Enough have been given concerning the more important issues to enable the reader to interpret the attitude of the court and the principles underlying the decision as made.

It has been considered necessary to include the detailed analysis of the important cases dealing with the subject of "Religion and the Bible in the Public Schools" as discussed in Chapter V. Citations have been given to the reports in which each case referred to may be found.

It has not been considered to be the purpose of this study to attempt to determine and report upon the history and treatment of each case. Nor has it been considered to be a part of the purpose of this study to attempt to determine what the law on the different issues discussed herein, is in any state to-day. Plainly, such a task would be far beyond the possibilities of this study. Constitutional provisions, statutory enactments, and case law differ so widely in the various states that such an attempt would be far beyond the reasonable compass of this study.

However, the name of the court making the decision and the date of the decision have been given in almost every instance. If the decision discussed has not been finally decisive of the case, this fact has been mentioned and the result of the appeal as to the issues pertinent to this study given. In some instances mention has been made of the fact that a decision has later been followed, distinguished, explained, or criticized. Where it has been deemed important, the fact that there was a dissenting opinion given by some member of the court has been noted and oftentimes a quotation from such opinion given. If a principle of law, pertinent to this study and applied in a case discussed here, has been later overruled, mention has been made of that fact. The citators accompanying the various reporter systems of the several states have been used in connection with each case discussed.

Noticeable trends in the decisions have been given at the close of each chapter dealing with original data. A summary has also been made for each of these chapters.

THE PLACE OF JUDICIAL DECISIONS IN THE LAW

The decision of a court of final resort is considered as establishing the rule of that jurisdiction upon the issues presented. While there is nothing to prevent the court from changing or completely reversing its position at any time on any issue that may come before it, nevertheless, it is usually very reluctant to do so unless there is strong evidence that the position previously assumed was erroneous or inequitable, or unless conditions have so changed as to warrant a change in the attitude of the court.

Concerning the responsibility of the courts for making law, Dr. Hicks * ¹ of Columbia University, in his book *Materials and Methods of Legal Research,* says:

The most that can be said is that by interpretation and amplification of statutes, courts operate coördinately with legislatures in law-making, and determine the detailed content of legislation. That courts do, coördinately with legislatures, and limited like them by constitutions, make law, seems now to be widely agreed upon.

As to the power of Courts and legislatures, the Illinois Supreme Court ² has declared:

Legislative power is the power to enact laws or to declare what the law shall be. Judicial power is the power which adjudicates upon the rights of citizens and to that end construes and applies the law.

In commenting upon the relation between the courts and the legislature the Supreme Court of West Virginia ³ in 1887 said in part:

It is the province of the courts to decide what the law is, and determine its application to particular facts, in the decision of causes. The province of the legislature is to declare what the law shall be in the future and neither of these departments can lawfully invade the province of the other.

The United States Supreme Court ⁴ in answer to the question as to the power of the legislature has used this language:

* Note: Footnotes will be numbered 1, 2, 3, as above. Citations will be numbered [1], [2], [3], etc., and will be found at the end of the chapter.

¹ Hicks, Frederick C., *Materials and Methods of Legal Research,* p. 32.
² Mitchell v. Lowden, 123 N.E. (Ill.) 566.
³ Shepard v. Wheeling, 30 W. Va. 479.
⁴ Knox v. Lee, Legal Tender Cases, 12 Wall. 457.

The answer is, the legislative department, being the nation itself, speaking by its representatives, has a choice of methods, and is the master of its own discretion.

DEFINITIONS AND TERMS USED

The word "curriculum" is used in this study as a general term by which to designate all the subject matter of instruction to which the child is exposed as a result of his school experience.

The term "judicial decision" has been used to refer to the decisions rendered by the regular courts of the land and also to the decisions made by the chief educational officer of the State of New York.[5]

This official was given the authority by statute in 1822 to hear and determine all questions in controversy which might arise in the administration of the common school system of New York.[6]

The courts have constantly sustained this power of this official.[7] They have held that his decisions, in all cases within his jurisdiction, are "final and conclusive and not subject to question or review in any place or court whatever," except in a

cause of action on the part of a taxpayer for an improper use of the funds and property of the board of education or the determination of constitutional questions or illegal acts on the part of officials.

An effort has been made to avoid as far as possible all technical legal terminology. However, it has been necessary to make use of technical terms at times in order to convey accurately the meaning intended.

The term "constitutional law" has been used to designate the fundamental or basic law as contained in the constitution of the United States and the constitutions of the several states. The term "statutory law" has been used to refer particularly to the acts of Congress and the acts of the state legislatures. Use has been made of the term "common law" to designate that body of law which has developed from custom and practice of the courts,

[5] In 1904 the title of this official was changed to that of Commissioner of Education. Previous to that date he had the title of State Superintendent of Public Instruction. Still earlier the title was that of State Superintendent of Common Schools.

[6] Finegan, *Judicial Decisions of the State Superintendent of Common Schools,* page 5.

[7] Stein v. Brown, 211 N. Y. S. 822.

the precedents for which are not contained in constitutions or statutes. The term "higher courts" has been used as a general term to indicate those state courts that have either appellate or final jurisdiction as distinguished from the usual county courts which have been referred to in a few instances as courts of "inferior" jurisdiction.

PREVIOUS STUDIES RELATING TO THE LAW AND THE CURRICULUM

Dr. J. K. Flanders [8] published a study in 1925 which gave the results of an investigation made by him to determine the nature and extent of legislative control of the elementary curriculum. He studied the prescriptions contained in the constitutions and statutes in force in the various states at three different periods, 1903, 1913, and 1923.

Dr. Arthur J. Hall [9] made a historical study dealing with religious education in New York. It was published in 1914. This study presented evidences of the place which religion had in the public schools of the state from the time of the first public schools until the date of the study.

Professor Harry R. Trusler [10] has published a series of magazine articles covering the period from 1913 to 1925 in which he has dealt with the law as related to various phases of education. Many of these articles touch upon the curriculum and some practices which relate to the instruction given in the public schools.

Charles N. Lischka [11] prepared a book in 1924 for the National Catholic Welfare Conference which contains the text and a classified summary of all state laws and constitutional provisions governing private schools in 1924. It also contains state constitutional and legislative provisions and some important judicial decisions dealing particularly with Bible reading in the public schools.

William R. Hood [12] has prepared a series of bulletins for the United States Bureau of Education during the period since 1913 and dealing particularly with the law in relation to education in general in the various states.

[8] Flanders, Jesse K., *Legislative Control of the Elementary Curriculum.*
[9] Hall, Arthur J., *Religious Education in the Public Schools of the State and City of New York.*
[10] See Bibliography, pages 167 and 168.
[11] Lischka, Charles N. (Compiler), *Private Schools and State Laws.*
[12] See Bibliography, page 166.

THE LIMITATIONS OF THE STUDY

Let it be said that no attempt has been made to advise the reader as to what the law is in any jurisdiction to-day. No reader is warranted in depending upon this study to determine his legal rights once he has become involved in a legal controversy. However, it is believed that this study will furnish a source of facts and will point out certain underlying and fundamental principles that should prove helpful to the thinking of those who are interested in the improvement and change of the curriculum of the public common schools.

CHAPTER II

JUDICIAL DECISIONS RELATING TO THE SCOPE OF THE CURRICULUM OF THE PUBLIC COMMON SCHOOLS

Shall the scope of the curriculum of the public common schools continue to be expanded? Shall the public school system provide adult education for all who wish it? Would the different state constitutions and statutes permit such education? The courts, through their construction of constitutional and statutory provisions and common-law rights, have been large factors in the shaping and formulating of the policies that have governed the development of the public school systems of our states. A knowledge of the attitude of the courts upon the issue of the progressive widening of the curriculum offered in the public schools is important to those who are interested in the public schools.

WHAT CONSTITUTES A PUBLIC COMMON SCHOOL?

The statutes and constitutions of the several states have usually made frequent use of the terms "public schools" and "common schools." The courts have had to determine the meaning of these terms many times. As attempts were made to extend the program of studies and to add other units of organization to educational systems there were those who made strenuous objections to such increases in the scope of the curriculum of the public schools.

The Massachusetts Supreme Judicial Court began to define the term "public school" by a decision [1] in 1832. This decision established two points; namely, (1) that the term "public school" could not be confined to those schools that were supported exclusively by municipal taxes for the reason that the legislature for some years had made grants of funds for the support of local schools, (2) that the term "public schools" could not be limited to schools supported "wholly by the public" for it properly included schools which derive support from voluntary

9

contributions as well as from public funds. Attention is here called to the fact that many courts have upheld gifts or devises for the purpose of instituting, endowing, or maintaining [2] a public school. They support such devises and gifts as being gifts for charitable purposes, or as creating a public charitable trust.

The Massachusetts Supreme Judicial Court added to this definition [3] in 1845. A town had provided such schools as were specifically required by law. In addition it had established and was maintaining a high school for girls. This high school was teaching bookkeeping, algebra, geometry, history, rhetoric, mental, moral and natural philosophy, botany, Latin, French, and other higher branches of knowledge than were taught in the grammar schools of the town. It was contended that such a school was not a public school. The Court held that this was a "town" school within the meaning of the statute and that the money collected by taxes for its support had been legally raised.

The Massachusetts Supreme Judicial Court further clarified thinking relative to the meaning of "public schools" in 1869. In this case [4] a man had left a will providing for the erection and maintenance of a free school. The will specified that certain of the trustees of this school, although to be selected by the electors of the district, must be chosen from the membership of certain churches. The building burned and there were not sufficient funds to rebuild and maintain the school. The town proposed that, as this school was for the free use of all people of the town, it would be economical and wise to consider it a public school and to assist in rebuilding and maintaining it with public funds. Objections arose. The Court laid down the rule that for a school to be a "public school" it is necessary that it be "under the order and superintendence" of the public. The Court explained that the requirement in the will that certain of the trustees must belong to particular churches took this case outside the rule and that, therefore, the school was not a public school and public money could not be used to assist it. This case also held that "common schools" and "public schools" were synonymous terms.

The Illinois Supreme Court [5] in 1881, in deciding whether the local school authorities might add modern languages to their curriculum under a statute which provided that instruction be given in the common or free schools in certain branches,

and in such other branches, including vocal music and drawing, as the directors, or voters of the district, at the annual election of directors may prescribe,

said in part:

Without being able to give any accurate definition of a "common school," it is safe to say the common understanding is, it is a school that begins with the rudimental elements of an education, whatever else it may embrace, as contra-distinguished from academies or universities devoted exclusively to the teaching of advanced pupils in the classics, and in all the higher branches of study usually included in the curriculum of the colleges.

In 1879 the Missouri Appellate Court [6] was called upon to define what was meant by "common schools" in the constitutional provision which required that the legislature provide a system of "common schools." This Court held that the word there meant "open to all, belonging to the public." This case was appealed to the Missouri Supreme Court [7] and in deciding it in 1883 that Court declared that in the legislation on that subject the schools were called "public" as often as "common" schools; that the words seemed to be used interchangeably as meaning one and the same thing. This Court considered that the term "common schools" meant "schools open and public to all" rather than schools of any definite grade. In the same decision the Court said that the term "school," by and of itself, does not imply a restriction to the rudiments of an education; that when contrasted with the term "college" or "university" it might and ordinarily did imply a lower grade, but just where the one ended and the other began might not be easy to determine. There are a number of states whose courts have held [8] that "common schools" and "public schools" mean "free schools."

WHAT SUBJECTS MAY BE TAUGHT IN THE COMMON SCHOOLS?

Not a case has been found in which the court decided against the offering of any secular subject in the public common schools, unless the teaching of such subject had already been prohibited by statute as in the case of the foreign languages, particularly German.

In 1874 the Michigan Supreme Court laid down the rule [9] that there was nothing in the constitution or the statutes to prevent local school boards from providing instruction in the classics and the modern languages in the Primary School Districts of Michigan. This early case has been followed in Michigan and cited in many other jurisdictions. Under substantially similar conditions, the Missouri decisions [6 and 7] and the Illinois decision [5], already referred to, were to the same effect as the Michigan decision. Under the same general conditions the Kentucky Court of Appeals in 1887 held [10] that Latin and Greek might be taught in the common schools of that state.

The Kansas Supreme Court [11] decided in 1893 that, while the law "prescribes" that certain subjects shall be taught in the common schools of the state, it "permits" other branches, including Latin and modern languages, to be taught. That Court's position was that the subjects prescribed by the state constituted only a required "minimum program" of studies that might be supplemented by the local school corporation of a first class city. In 1916 the Kansas Supreme Court [11] went still further and held that, under the statute, the school district boards might provide for other branches than those enumerated in the statute, including music, and that, furthermore, a special teacher might be employed to teach this subject in one or more schools of the district.

The decisions of the chief educational officer of the State of New York have gone far in upholding the power of the local school authorities, under the statutes giving local school corporations general powers to conduct their schools, to add to their curriculum. In 1888 the power [12] of a local school corporation to raise funds for the teaching of vocal music was upheld. In 1919 the Commissioner [13] held that a local school district board might add a course in domestic science to its curriculum; that in connection with this course it might establish a free lunch system for the children taking the course; that it might do these things although no appropriation of funds had been made by the district voters for them. In 1920 he decided [14] that the teaching of "speech improvement," as applied to the correction of speech defects such as stammering, stuttering, and kindred ailments, is a "special subject" which may be taught in the public schools and that specially trained teachers may be hired to do this work.

The power of local school authorities to provide the study of music, under the general powers conferred upon them by statute, has been frequently attacked. In addition to the decisions concerning this subject already discussed, the Supreme Court of Iowa [15] in 1876 upheld the power of the local authorities to provide for the study of music. The Indiana Supreme Court [16] did likewise in 1886 and affirmed its position in 1901.

The Supreme Court of Illinois [17] upheld the local school board's power to establish the study of bookkeeping by a decision given in 1875. The Court declared that, under the statute which invested the school board with general powers to establish and control the schools, the board might add bookkeeping to the list of studies prescribed by statute; but that it could not expel a pupil for refusing, under the directions of his or her father, to take that study.

In 1910 the Supreme Court of Wisconsin [18] held that, under the Wisconsin statute and an ordinance of the city in question, the school corporation of Oshkosh might provide for the teaching of manual training to all the pupils of the city and that it might erect and maintain one or more buildings exclusively for the teaching of manual training.

The Indiana Supreme Court [19] declared in 1919 that the statutes of Indiana were broad enough to permit the school trustees to arrange for field day exercises for their schools and hold them on school time.

Dancing as a part of the curriculum in physical education—which the statute required to be taught—was upheld as an addition to the curriculum by a local board in a decision [20] made by the California Supreme Court in 1922.

IS A GRADED SCHOOL A COMMON SCHOOL?

When those who were interested in better schools insisted upon graded schools for children, objections were sometimes made that such "graded" schools were not "common" schools such as were contemplated by constitutions and statutes and, therefore, could not be conducted with common school funds. Kentucky has a line of cases [21] on this question, beginning in 1888 and ending in 1910. They hold that "graded" schools are common schools; that simply because there is a desire to have better schools with more teachers in charge does not mean that the character of such schools as "common" schools is thereby affected.

IS THE HIGH SCHOOL A PART OF THE COMMON SCHOOL?

Opponents of the public high school sought in many jurisdictions to have the courts declare that the curriculum of the common schools could not legally be extended to include this additional unit of school organization. The legality of raising funds by public taxation to support and maintain a girls' high school was decided in a Massachusetts case [3] in 1845. It was contended that such funds could not legally be raised to teach higher branches of knowledge than were taught in the grammar schools of the town. However, the court decided that such a school could properly be maintained by taxes. In 1874 the Michigan Supreme Court [9] was called upon to decide this question. This Court decided that a school district had a statutory right to levy taxes upon the general public to support high schools wherein tuition was free and this too when free instruction of children in other languages than the English was provided.

In 1877 the Illinois Supreme Court [22] had this same general question before it. It held that it was the object of the law which allowed high schools to be established by townships "to afford increased facilities for acquiring a good education in free schools." This Court further held that the trustees of high schools had the same duties as directors of district schools and that their powers were governed by the same law. In 1904 the same Court [23] held that, under the Illinois constitution, which required that the General Assembly should provide a "thorough and efficient system of free schools whereby all children of the state might receive a good common school education," and the statute which sought to carry out the constitutional provision, any school district might establish and maintain a high school department. Again, in 1909, the Illinois Supreme Court [24] passed upon this question and this time it strengthened the rule by holding that, where a high school is a department of the common schools, the children of the district hold no different relation to the high school than that sustained to any other grade or department of the district schools, since the entire system of schools together constitutes the "common schools" of the district. The same Court [25] held in 1914 that a "good common school education," as mentioned in the Illinois constitution when providing for a free system of common schools, is not limited to the primary or intermediate grade, but may be extended to include a high school education.

The constitution in force in Kansas in 1890 required that the legislature establish a "uniform system of common schools and schools of higher grade, embracing normal, preparatory, collegiate, and university departments." The first case to come before the Supreme Court grew out of a law which provided for the establishment of county high schools in certain counties. Opponents of the high school contended that the constitution did not authorize the establishment of high schools at all. The Supreme Court [26] held in 1890 that such county high schools fell within that class of schools authorized by the constitution because such high schools were "schools of a higher grade" rather than "common schools"; that even if it were not so, there was nothing in the constitution which prohibited their establishment. This seems to have been a departure from the position taken by most other courts. However, this case may be distinguished owing to the fact that it arose under this special law for the establishment of county schools.

In 1893 the Kansas Supreme Court [11] faced squarely the issue of whether or not the high school is a part of the common school and declared that, although the statute then in question was entitled "An Act for the Regulation and Support of Common Schools," the legislature included therein "high schools" as a part of the uniform system of "public schools." This Court further said:

Under our liberal and beneficent system of public schools, we perceive no good reason why the higher branches prescribed by the board of education of the city of Topeka may not in its discretion be taught in the public schools, and no good reason why scholars desiring to be instructed in such branches may not be provided with a separate school building, properly furnished, whether it be called a "public school," a "graded school," or a "high school."

The same Court [27] in 1904 decided that the high school grade of a city school system was a part of the common school system. In 1924 the same Court [28] held that the ninth grade, under the Kansas educational system, was a high school grade, even in cities that have junior high schools and organize their schools after the plan of six years of elementary work, three years of intermediate work, and three years of senior high school work.

The Commissioner of Education of New York and the Supreme Courts of Georgia, Arkansas, and North Carolina [29] have held that high schools that are being publicly maintained for free instruction for all children are "free common schools" within the meaning of the statutes and the state constitutions.

Upon first consideration it would seem that a few courts have taken the position that the high school is not to be considered as a part of the common school. However, these cases can be distinguished from the cases holding in line with the majority of the courts. The California Appellate Court [30] in 1906 held that the political code regulating the government of high schools was not to be controlled by the provisions of the code applicable to the common schools. The California Supreme Court [31] has held in at least two cases that high schools are not a part of the primary and grammar school system. The position of these courts is made clear by this statement [31] by the Supreme Court in 1905:

> The "common" or "free school" is made the special and exclusive beneficiary of the state school fund and the school tax, but all the enumerated educational instrumentalities (primary, kindergarten, grammar, evening, and high school) belong to our public school system and may be authorized and their support provided for by the legislature.

The need of including the high school in the term "common school" in order to legalize the high school did not occur in California, since the constitution itself provided for the high school.

The Supreme Court of Idaho in 1911 decided a case [32] involving the interpretation of the term "schools" as used in the Idaho constitution. It was held that the term as therein used referred to the

> public, free, common schools generally adopted in the country, and having special reference to the district schools throughout the state

established for the training and instruction of the youth in the elementary branches of learning below the grade of academy, seminary, college, university, or other literary or scientific institution.

This was not really an interpretation of the term "common schools." It was rather a construction of what class of schools the legislature intended to include in a statute that prohibited the use of public funds to aid any church or religious society in its support of any school, academy, seminary, college, or other literary or scientific institution. This Court later used the term "public schools" to refer to "all public educational institutions."

The Missouri legislature in 1889 chartered a corporation called "The Bridgeton Academy." The charter provided that, "in addition to the branches taught in the common schools of the state, Latin and higher branches of mathematics should be taught in the academy." The legality of this corporation was attacked upon various points but the Court held [33] it to be a legal public corporation. However, the wording as to "common schools" quoted above is not legally significant because it was not an issue of the case, and too, the Missouri Court has held in other decisions [7] that the high school is a part of the common school.

The Commissioner of Education of New York has decided not less than twenty cases [34] since 1916 in which the rule was laid down that the local school corporation is under the necessity of providing high school instruction for its children since high schools, being publicly maintained for the free instruction of all children, are "free common schools" within the meaning of the constitution.

Does a law requiring that high school education be provided by the local board constitute class legislation and as such is it unconstitutional? The Supreme Courts of Tennessee and Minnesota [35] answered that question in the negative as late as 1923.

A question that assumed some importance in recent years, but which has gone up to the supreme court in only one state, grew out of the desire of school corporations to build gymnasiums as separate buildings in which to hold the athletic contests of the high school. The Vermont Supreme Court [36] in 1925 held that the city of Burlington had acted within its statutory authority in providing, in a separate building, a gymnasium in connection with the high school and this too on a plot of ground owned by the civil city.

ARE KINDERGARTENS A PART OF THE COMMON SCHOOL SYSTEM?

Those who opposed the extension of the scope of the curriculum of the public schools attacked the kindergarten as well as the high school. The constitution in effect in Missouri in 1879 provided that the "General Assembly shall establish and maintain free public schools, for the gratuitous instruction of all persons in this state between the ages of six and twenty years." In a case [6] before the Missouri Appellate Court in 1879 it was sought to restrain the St. Louis public school corporation from expending public funds for the education of children below the age of six years. This Court decided that from whatever source the public school funds come they must be expended in accord with the provisions of existing legislation and subject to the provisions of the existing constitution; that the provisions of the constitution as quoted above constituted a requirement that the legislature provide for the education of all persons between the ages of six and twenty years of age; that this did not amount to a prohibition which prevented the instruction of persons who were not between the ages of six and twenty. This case [7] was before the Missouri Supreme Court in 1883 on appeal, and the Court held that the constitution forbade the expenditure of school funds for the education of children below the age of six years, thus reversing that part of the Appellate Court's decision [6]. This decision was based solely upon the constitutional provision as to age and not upon the kind or nature of the work done in the kindergarten. This Court simply held that the constitution set the limits for the expenditure of public funds for public education at the years from six to twenty and that expenditures for the education of those below six were illegal, being unconstitutional.

The reader may be interested in knowing that in 1913 the legislature of Missouri passed an act [37] providing that:

The Board of Directors or Board of Education of any school district in this state may provide for the gratuitous education of persons between four and six, and over 20 years of age, resident in such school district. Such gratuitous education, however, shall be provided only out of revenues other than those described in Section 6, Art. XI, of the Constitution of this state, and only with so much of such revenues as are not required for the establishing and maintaining of free public schools in such school districts for the gratuitous instruction of persons between the ages of six and 20 years: Provided that nothing in this section shall be construed as affecting the basis of apportionment of the public school fund of this state as now fixed by law.

The Supreme Court of Missouri has not passed upon the constitutionality of this act.

In 1893 the Colorado Supreme Court [38] followed the reasoning and the decision of the Missouri Appellate Court [6] as to the education of children below the age of six. In 1915 the Arkansas Supreme Court [29] followed the decision of the Missouri Supreme Court [7] on the same question. The constitutional provisions were similar in each case.

In California the matter came before the Supreme Court [39] in a little different form. California had made use of the term "primary school system" in providing for the lower part of her school system. The court was asked to decide whether or not the kindergarten might be established as a part of this "primary school system" and it so held.

ARE TEACHER-TRAINING DEPARTMENTS OR SCHOOLS A PART OF THE COMMON SCHOOL SYSTEM?

High School Teacher-Training Departments. The Supreme court of Arkansas [29] in 1915 held that, under the provisions of the constitution of the state, high schools in which normal school training is given are a part of the common school system.

State Normal Schools. In the case just cited [29], the Supreme Court decided that separate normal schools are not a part of the common school system. The Supreme Courts of Missouri [40] and North Dakota [41] have held that the constitutions of the respective states provide for the state normal school as a part of the "free public school system." These decisions do not say that such schools are a part of the "common school system." The Supreme Court of Washington [42] plainly says that, under the constitution, a normal school is not a "common school."

The Model Training School. In the case just cited [42] the Court held that the model training school department of a normal school is not a part of the common schools of the state and that money from the state common school fund may not be applied to the support of such model training school department of a normal school. The test applied here was that the model training school was not under the "control of the school district"; that since those in charge of the model training school might select the pupils who should enter, it was not "common to all of a proper age." In a later case [43] this same Court held that the attendance of children at a model training school conducted by the state normal school could not, under the statute, be counted in determining the apportionment of funds to a county from the current common school funds of the state.

The Supreme Court of Iowa [44] in 1919 held that school trustees who permitted normal school students to do practice teaching in the public schools under the supervision of a public school teacher and without compensation, were not abusing their authority by permitting the establishment and conduct of a school of pedagogy in the public school building.

New York seems to have gone further on this point than any other state. The Superintendent of that state in 1891 held [45] that the legislature had power to provide that a district school might become a normal training school and that the district organization might cease to exist and all moneys coming due to such district should be paid over to the normal school.

The Supreme Court of West Virginia [46] in 1914 held that, under the statutes of West Virginia, the school district of Fairmont was authorized to establish and maintain a teacher-training department.

ARE EVENING SCHOOLS A PART OF THE PUBLIC COMMON SCHOOL SYSTEM?

Two interesting questions are raised in connection with the evening school. Even though the course of an evening high school extends over a period of five years, does the school still have a right to participate in the state distribution of funds? The California Supreme Court [47] in 1915 decided this question in the affirmative. May the statute set up a certain minimum of requirements as to the number of teachers, periods per day, etc., which the evening school must meet in order to participate in the state distribution of funds? The same case also answered this question in the affirmative. The Court did not need to decide whether or not the evening school was a part of the common school system. The California constitution itself provides that the public school system shall include primary and grammar schools, and such high schools, evening schools, commercial schools and technical schools as may be established by the legislature or municipal or district authority. The words "evening school" were here merely intended to obviate doubt as to the power [47] to provide for schools holding evening sessions and of course the constitution would not prevent the conduct of an evening high school as a part of the public school system. The construction of the words "common schools" is therefore not necessary in California in order to settle this question. However, the evening school is included in that part of the public school system that is recognized in all the states as a part of the common school system.

ARE VOCATIONAL SCHOOLS A PART OF THE PUBLIC COMMON SCHOOL SYSTEM?

Opponents of the extension of the curriculum of the public schools have opposed vocational schools and departments as being illegal or unconstitutional. The Minnesota Court [48] held in 1913 that the legislature had power under the constitution to require that education be given beyond the common branches and that it might also require instruction in the subjects of agriculture and home economics. The Kansas Supreme Court [49] in the same year took the position that the authority which school boards had to acquire land for "sites" for school buildings, playgrounds, or additions and extensions thereto, did not authorize them to purchase land for use in teaching vocational agriculture.

THE SCOPE OF THE PUBLIC COMMON SCHOOL IN GENERAL

In 1879 the Missouri Appellate Court [6] held that the St. Louis School Board was not limited by its charter to any grade of instruction; that although the St. Louis schools were a part of the state school system the city board was not governed by such provisions of the general school laws as were clearly not intended to apply to it.

In 1880 the State Superintendent of New York [50] decided

that the subjects to be taught in common schools may be determined by the trustees and that their determination will not be interfered with unless it is an abuse of discretion on their part. In 1923 the New York Supreme Court [51] held that the section of the New York constitution which said that "the legislature shall provide for the maintenance and support of a system of free common schools, wherein all the children of this state may be educated" is not a limitation of authority which prevents the legislature from exceeding its terms, but is the imposition of a duty which fixes the minimum of compliance. This case [52] is one of several which grew out of an attempt to prevent the city of New York from continuing to maintain the College of the City of New York and Hunter College of the City of New York on the grounds that the constitution limited free education to the common schools. The Court upheld the maintenance of these schools.

The New Jersey Supreme Court [53] stated its position in 1904 as follows:

The facilities for free public education are to be provided by the legislature, within the exercise of a sound discretion, subject only to constitutional restraints, which must be found in clear expressions or implications.

In 1898 the Illinois Appellate Court [54] held that the board of education of a township high school had the duties of school directors to specify what branches of study should be taught and this without the vote of the district; also to establish instruction in such other branches as they might prescribe, including manual training. The Illinois Supreme Court [55] in 1914 held that a "good common school education," as contemplated by the Illinois constitution, was not limited to the primary, or the intermediate grade, but might be extended to include a high school education, the high school being as much a part of the free schools as the district school. This decision [56] has since been followed. In 1922 the same Court [57] held that, under the Illinois constitution, which requires the legislature to provide a "common school education," the legislature had unquestioned power and discretion to determine what a "common school education" should be.

The Minnesota Court [58] held in 1910 that a school board might employ a suitable person to ascertain the physical condition of the pupils of the public schools.

The New York State Superintendent in 1891 held [59] that the school board might allow its building to be used to give instruction in music to a band composed of pupils of the school.

The Kentucky Court of Appeals [60] decided that the printing and the furnishing of manuals on such subjects as "Arbor and Bird Day," "Bulletins on Home Economics," etc., were not authorized by the statute which directed the state superintendent to make a biennial report on the common schools, and to give such other facts, statistics, and information as may be deemed of interest to be known.

THE TREND OF THE DECISIONS

The general trend of the decisions undoubtedly has been toward favoring definitely the widening of the scope of the curriculum of the public common schools. In the cases discussed in this chapter it is possible to determine one hundred twenty-one instances where this issue has been passed upon by the courts. In one hundred instances the court decided in favor of widening the curriculum and in twenty-one instances the decision was against it. Eight of these unfavorable instances involved the question of whether or not the common school might be connected with a sectarian school and eight of them involved the issue of whether the normal school was to be considered a part of the common school or not.

A definite trend of the decisions can be determined in the case of the following specific issues:

1. What is the meaning of a "public common school"? This trend goes from a totally undefined conception of the term toward the development of a broad inclusive definition of that expression.

2. What subjects may be taught in the common schools? The trend is toward the recognition of the right of the legislature or the local school corporation, unless expressly prohibited by the legislature, to add at their discretion any secular subject whatever to the curriculum.

3. Is the high school a part of the common school? The trend has always been decidedly in favor of legalizing, whenever it has been questioned, the introduction of the high school by holding it to be a part of the common school for which so many state constitutions made provision without specifically providing for high schools.

4. What is the power of the local school authorities to use the public common schools for model training school purposes? Although the decisions are divided the trend seems to be toward the favoring of such use.

SUMMARY

I. The courts' conception of what constitutes a "public common school" includes the following points:
1. Terminology:
    a. "Public schools," "common schools," "free schools," are, in general, synonymous terms.
    b. The term "school," by and of itself, does not imply a restriction to the rudiments of an education.
    c. When contrasted with the term "college" or "university" the term "school" may and ordinarily does imply a lower grade, but just where the one leaves off and the other begins may not be clear.
2. Essential elements:
    a. Unhampered, unrestricted and complete public control.
    b. Free, open equally to all.
    c. No reference to the kind of studies taught.
3. Unjustifiable limitations:
    a. Restriction of support to local school corporation.
    b. Refusal to allow other than public support.

II. The courts have favored the introduction of any secular subject whatever into the common school curriculum except those specifically prohibited by act of the legislature.

III. Graded schools are held to be "common schools."

IV. The courts have held the high school to be a part of the common school in all instances where the existence of and maintenance of the high school have depended upon considering it to be a part of the common school system which has been provided for by the state constitutions.

V. The courts have been divided upon the issue of the kindergarten being a part of the common school system. The courts that have decided against the inclusion of the kindergarten have not done so because of any objection to the nature of the work done. The position taken has been that the constitution of the state restricted public education to certain age limits.

VI. Teacher-training departments or schools:

1. High school teacher-training departments have been held to be a part of the common school.

2. The courts have not stated their positions clearly on the status of normal schools and are divided. The general rule seems to be that normal schools are public schools in so far as their support and their acceptance of students are concerned but that they are not "common schools" in so far as to allow them to be supported from the state funds set aside for supporting elementary and high schools.

3. Model training schools, to be public common schools, must be free and open equally to all. Some states hold that these schools must be under the control of the school district, but New York has held that the funds and the control may both be handed over to the normal school.

VII. Evening schools have been held to be a part of the common school.

VIII. Although there has been some difference in the attitude of the courts, vocational schools that admit pupils of the same ages as those of the traditional schools are considered to be common schools.

IX. The courts take the following attitude toward the scope of the curriculum of the public common school in general:

1. The people may have put factors of restriction or control into the constitution and these must be respected.

2. The legislature may at its discretion extend or restrict the curriculum of the public common schools, provided such discretion does not conflict with constitutional provisions. The courts will not interfere with the exercise of such discretion unless it amounts to abuse.

3. The local school corporation may regulate the scope of its local curriculum at its discretion, provided only that it observe the provisions of the constitution and the legislature.

CITATIONS ON CHAPTER II

1. Allen v. School District, 15 Pick. (Mass.) 35.
2. Maxcy v. City of Oshkosh, 144 Wis. 238;
   Herron v. Stanton, 79 Ind. App. 683;

Hamburger v. Cornell University, 199 N. Y. S. 369;
Lupton v. Leander Clark College, 187 N. W. (Ia.) 496;
American Digest, Key-Number, Charities 12.
3. Cushing v. Inhabitants, 51 Mass. 508.
4. Jenkins v. Andover, 103 Mass. 94.
5. Powell v. Board, 97 Ill. 375.
6. Roach v. St. Louis, 7 Mo. App. 567.
7. Roach v. St. Louis, 77 Mo. 484.
8. Board v. Dick, 70 Kan. 434;
Jenkins v. Andover, 103 Mass. 94;
Merrick v. Amherst, 12 Allen (Mass.) 500, 509;
Collins v. Henderson, 74 Ky. 74;
Irom v. Gregory, 86 Ga. 605;
People v. Board, 13 Barb. (N. Y.) 400.
9. Stewart v. School District, 30 Mich. 69.
10. Newman v. Thompson, 4 S. W. (Ky.) 341.
11. Board v. Welch, 51 Kan. 792;
Epley v. Hall, 97 Kan. 549.
12. Finegan, Decisions New York Supt. 329.
13. 21 New York State Dept. Rep. 23.
14. 22 N. Y. St. Dept. Rep. 565.
15. Bellmeyer v. Independent Distr., 44 Ia. 564.
16. State v. Webber, 108 Ind. 31;
Meyers Pub. Co. v. White River District, 28 Ind. App. 91.
17. Rulison v. Post, 79 Ill. 567.
18. Maxcy v. City, 144 Wis. 238.
19. Adams v. Schneider, 124 N. E. (Ind.) 718.
20. Board v. Fruitridge, 205 Pac. (Cal.) 49.
21. Trustees v. Harrodsburg, 7 S. W. (Ky.) 312;
Williamstown Dist. v. Webb, 89 Ky. 264;
Riggs v. Stevens, 92 Ky. 393;
Jeffries v. Board, 135 Ky. 488.
22. Trustees v. People, 87 Ill. 303.
23. Russell v. High School Board, 212 Ill. 327.
24. People v. Moore, 240 Ill. 408.
25. Cook v. Directors, 266 Ill. 164.
26. Koester v. Board, 44 Kan. 141.
27. Board v. Dick, 70 Kan. 434.
28. Thurman-Watts v. Board, 222 P. (Kan.) 123.
29. 15 N. Y. St. Dept. Rep. 506;
Cumming v. Board, 175 U. S. 528, affirming Board v. Cumming, 103 Ga. 641;
Dickerson v. Edmondson, 120 Ark. 80;
Board of Ed. v. Board of Commissioners, 93 S. E. (N. C.) 1001.
30. Bancroft v. Randall, 4 Cal. App. 406.
31. People v. Lodi, 124 Cal. 694;
Macmillan Co. v. Clarke, 184 Cal. 491.
32. Pike v. State Board, 19 Idaho 268;

State v. Hoover, 19 Idaho 299.
33. State v. Vaughn, 99 Mo. 332.
34. 10 N. Y. St. Dept. Rep. 449;
22 N. Y. St. Dept. Rep. 577, 586, 713, 673, 740, 788, 796, 811;
26 N. Y. St. Dept. Rep. 46, 680;
27 N. Y. St. Dept. Rep. 544;
28 N. Y. St. Dept. Rep. 560;
29 N. Y. St. Dept. Rep. 292, 326, 409, 459, 622;
30 N. Y. St. Dept. Rep. 159, 703;
31 N. Y. St. Dept. Rep. 240, 455;
32 N. Y. St. Dept. Rep. 602.
35. State v. Smith, 254 S. W. (Tenn.) 554;
Curryer v. Merrill, 25 Minn. 1.
36. City of Burlington v. Mayor, 127 A. (Vt.) 892.
37. Missouri Laws 1913, page 717.
38. In Re Kindergarten Schools, 18 Colo. 234. This is merely an opinion
given upon request of the Legislature by the Supreme Court.
39. Sinnott v. Colombet, 107 Cal. 187.
40. Kayser v. Board, 273 Mo. 643.
41. State v. Valley City School, 173 N. W. (N. D.) 750;
see also Underwood v. Wood, 93 Ky. 177;
Collins v. Henderson, 74 Ky. 74;
Halbert v. Sparks, 72 Ky. 259;
Halls Free School v. Horne, 80 Va. 470.
42. School District v. Bryan, 51 Wash. 498.
43. State v. Preston, 79 Wash. 286.
44. Clay v. Independent Distr., 174 N. W. (Ia.) 47.
45. Finegan, Decisions N. Y. Supt. 418.
46. Spedden v. Board, 74 W. Va. 181.
47. Board v. Hyatt, 152 Cal. 515.
48. Associated Schools v. School District, 122 Minn. 254.
49. Board v. Davis, 90 Kan. 621.
50. Finegan, Decisions N. Y. Supt. 1294.
51. College v. Hylan, 199 N. Y. S. 804.
52. College v. Hylan, 199 N. Y. S. 634. This case criticises 190 N. Y. S.
405, 947. Supporting decisions cited are: 17 Pa. St. 118, 120; 91
Ky. 6, 18; 47 N. Y. 608, 618.
53. Trustees v. Morgan, 70 N. J. Law 460.
54. People v. Board, 176 Ill. App. 491.
55. Cook v. Board, 266 Ill. 164.
56. Swain v. Stewart, 267 Ill. 29;
People v. School Directors, 267 Ill. 172.
57. People v. Young, 309 Ill. 27.
58. State v. Brown, 122 Minn. 370.
59. Finegan, Decisions N. Y. Supt. 803.
60. Vansant v. Commonwealth, 189 Ky. 1.

CHAPTER III

JUDICIAL DECISIONS RELATING TO THE CONTROL OF THE CURRICULUM OF THE PUBLIC SCHOOLS BY LEGISLATIVE ACTION

A group of federated sovereign states established the present form of government for the United States of America by adopting the United States Constitution in 1789. The theory underlying the powers of the federal government is that it is a government of delegated powers; that all powers not delegated by the states to the federal government nor denied to the states are reserved by and for the separate states. The Constitution of the United States makes no provision for education. The word "education" does not even occur in it. By implication this power was exclusively reserved to the separate states. The legislation affecting education in the states that has been passed by Congress has been indirect and the effect secured through the use of land and money grants. Under the democratic theory of government as practiced in the United States, the voters are the sovereign power. They formulate and establish their state constitutions. The state constitution sets up the framework of the state government. This framework is made up of the legislative, executive, and judicial departments as is the case in the federal government. The constitution of each state makes it the duty of the legislative assembly of the state to establish, maintain, and control a system of public schools in the state.[1]

No cases have been found during the course of this study in which the constitutionality of the federal legislation providing for federal aid for vocational education has been determined.

It was explained in the Introduction to this study that it is the province of the legislative department of the government to enact laws and declare what the law shall be; that it is the function of the courts to decide what the law is and determine its application to particular facts in the decision of individual cases brought before them.

[1] Reisner, E. H., *Nationalism and Education Since 1789*, pp. 323-351.

DECISIONS RELATING TO LEGISLATIVE CONTROL IN GENERAL

The attention of the reader is called to the fact that throughout this study the control of the state legislature over the schools is constantly referred to and emphasized in the discussion of the cases which have arisen as a result of constitutional provisions and the statutory enactments of the legislature concerning its establishment, maintenance, and control of the schools. The decisions of the courts of the different states in construing the nature and extent of the state legislature's responsibility for and control of the state's schools, as well as in construing the laws passed by the legislature in seeking to perform its duties in connection with the school system, show the extent to which the decisions of the courts play a part in determining and shaping the development of the state's school system and the curriculum of the schools. However, some specific and pointed quotations from several judicial decisions will emphasize the importance of the influence of the courts.

The Wisconsin Supreme Court [1] in 1923 used this language in a decision involving this issue:

In view of the fact that the Constitution is not a grant of, but a limitation upon, legislative power, the Legislature may adopt any measures which in its judgment will promote the efficiency of the schools of the State, unless prohibited by some express constitutional provision.

The Indiana Supreme Court has made a number of decisions which have emphasized the authority of the legislature over the public schools. This Court [2] expressed itself in 1889 as follows:

It has been the uniform course, since the organization of the State to regulate and control school affairs by legislation. · All public schools have been established under legislative enactments and all rules and regulations have been made pursuant to statutory authority. . . . Every school that has ever been established owes its existence to legislation; and every school officer owes his authority to the statute.

In 1924 this same Court [3] said:

It is for the legislature to determine through what agencies its power, under the constitution, to provide for a public school system shall be carried out, and how the burden shall be divided between local governmental units. . . . The power to provide for public schools, being a legislative one, is not exhausted by exercise, but the legislature may change plans as often as it deems necessary or expedient, and is answerable only to the people, not to the courts, for mistakes or abuses.

There are a number of Indiana cases [4] that are in agreement with this principle.

In a decision involving this issue and handed down in 1889 the Michigan Supreme Court [5] stated its position in part as follows:

The authority granted by the Constitution to the Legislature to establish a common primary school system carried with it the authority to prescribe what officers should be chosen to conduct the affairs of the school district, to define their powers and duties, their term of office, and how and by whom they should be chosen.

This same Court [6] in 1922 used this language:

Subject only to the Constitution, providing that schools and the means of education shall forever be encouraged, and also providing that primary schools shall be maintained in every district in the State for the education of its pupils without charge for tuition, the legislature has entire control over the schools of the State and their operation.

In 1893 the Colorado Supreme Court [7] made this declaration:

Unless the Constitution in express terms or by necessary implication limits it, the legislature may exercise its sovereign power in any way that, in its judgment, will best subserve the general welfare.

A number of cases [8] have been found in agreement with this position.

The California Supreme Court [9] in 1920 made the strongest statement that this study has revealed on this issue:

The presumption which attends every act of the legislature is that it is within the constitutional power. . . . The legislature is vested with the whole of the legislative power of the state and may deal with any subject within the scope of civil government, unless it is restrained by provision of the constitution.

In discussing the power which the legislature had given to a local school board the Missouri Appellate Court [10] in 1879 declared:

The courts have no power to prescribe what shall or shall not be taught in the public schools of Missouri.

DECISIONS RELATING TO THE ELEMENTS OF A UNIFORM SYSTEM OF COMMON SCHOOLS

The courts of some of the states have made some interesting rulings which show their conception of the elements that are included in the term "uniform system of public schools." The Supreme Court of Montana [11] in 1896 held that the provision of the constitution that "It shall be the duty of the legislative assembly of Montana to establish and maintain a general uniform and thorough system of public, free common schools" did not make it necessary that the textbooks used in the schools should be uniform throughout the State in order that there should be "a uniform system of schools."

In 1903 the Mississippi Supreme Court [12] declared unconstitutional a statute which designated certain persons as trustees of one particular public school to serve for a term of twenty years; which gave the trustees power to fill vacancies in their number and exclusive control of the school, together with other powers not conferred by the general laws on trustees of public schools in other instances. The Court said in part:

. . . Section 6 of said act of 1888 not only provides for induction into office of the trustees, but confers upon them most peculiar and extraordinary powers—powers wholly different from the powers conferred upon trustees of common schools by the general law in force at that time or now. The purpose of the Constitution of 1869, declaring that it should be the duty of the legislature to establish a uniform system of public schools, was to make the system uniform in all that related to the executive administration of the common schools of the state. The purpose was to secure a uniform administration of the common schools. It was meant that the "system" should be administered uniformly, on a uniform plan, the same throughout the state. It is impossible to conceive how there can be any such uniform system where the trustees of some of the common schools are chosen in the mode provided for in the general law and vested only with certain powers therein prescribed, carefully limited and defined and the trustees of others,—confessedly public schools, parts of the common school "system"—are not only chosen in a wholly different way from that in which other trustees are chosen, but are given the power to perpetuate themselves indefinitely, also practically the power of taxation and other powers not conferred upon trustees selected under the general law. The object of the Constitution was perfectly clear, and no amount of statement can either make it plainer or obscure that plainly declared purpose.

The Supreme Court of Georgia [13] in 1904 declared unconstitutional a special act of the legislature which incorporated as a district a part of a county which was not included in a town or city and gave it different powers than were given to school districts under the general law concerning the establishing and organizing of school districts. The Court said:

> Whatever may be the right of a county, city or town to establish special or local systems, the constitution grants no power to the General Assembly to authorize the establishment and maintenance of a special or local school system in a rural district. . . . It declares that "there shall be a thorough system of common schools for the education of children in the elementary branches of an English education only, as nearly uniform as practicable, the expenses of which shall be provided by taxation or otherwise." The constitution prohibits the destruction of this uniformity.

The Minnesota Supreme Court [14] presented a holding on still another point of interest in regard to uniformity. In 1913 it held that the legislature had power to impose a system of public education which was not limited to common branches alone; that it could require that school corporations that did not maintain high schools and schools that taught agriculture and home economics, should pay the tuition of their children who went to other schools in order to obtain such education; that this provision was not a violation of the constitutional requirement for a "uniform system of public schools."

RELATING TO SOME SPECIFIC CONTROLS BY THE STATE LEGISLATURE

The Determination of What System of Education to Use

The Kentucky Court of Appeals [15] in 1909 held that a statute which, among other things, changed the Kentucky system outside of the graded schools, substituting the county unit system for the district trustee system, was constitutional. The Court expressed itself in part as follows:

> The Constitution requires the General Assembly to provide by appropriate legislation an efficient system of common schools throughout

the State. What system will be most efficient is for the judgment of the General Assembly. . . . In a matter like this, resting within the discretion of the General Assembly, the court will not substitute its judgment for the judgment of the Assembly, and will not interfere with the action of the Legislature, unless a palpable effort to evade the mandate of the Constitution should appear.

The New York Supreme Court [16] in 1903 held that, under the Charter of Greater New York "which conferred on the board of education the power to establish and conduct elementary schools, kindergartens, manual training schools, trade schools, truant schools, evening schools and vacation schools," the evening school is just as much a part of the common school system in Greater New York as is an elementary school. This case [17], which primarily involved the right of the board of education to deprive a male principal of an evening school of his position after the board had determined to change his evening school into an evening school exclusively for girls with a lady principal, was reversed by the New York Court of Appeals. It was later heard again by the Supreme Court [18] but in none of the cases was the right denied to the legislature of giving to a class of cities into which New York falls the right to have and establish this special kind of school.

In construing the various statutes dealing with the State's legislation concerning the public schools the North Dakota Supreme Court [19] in 1920 expressed the following opinion in part:

Apparently no one has ever questioned the right of the Legislature to so exercise this power of regulation (of the public school system). There is in fact no doubt that it possesses this power, not only by reason of no restrictive provision inhibiting the exercise of such power in the Constitution, but by direct mandate so to do therein. There is, furthermore, no question that this power of the Legislature extends to the right to prescribe courses of study or subjects to be taught in the public schools.

The Indiana Supreme Court [2] took a similar position in 1889.

Prescription of Courses of Study

(1) *In General.* It has already been pointed out that the courts have no direct power to prescribe [10] the curriculum of the public schools. It has also been shown by the numerous

citations and quotations in this chapter that, except for restrictions by the federal and state constitutions, the legislature not only has the power but is also charged with the duty and obligation of establishing, maintaining, and controlling the public school system in its state. The attitude of the courts toward this power and duty of the legislature is shown by these decisions. In Chapter II of this study the decisions of the courts relating to the scope of the curriculum and the legislature's part in widening and extending it were discussed. As a part of the legislature's complete control of the public school system, the control of the curriculum of these schools seems but an inherent incident. However quoting some cases where the courts have recognized and emphasized this power of the legislature may be worth while. Several cases have been found in which this issue has been directly raised and decided, while many cases have indirectly raised this issue.

In 1881 the Illinois Supreme Court [20] in construing the right of the legislature, under the constitution, to determine what subjects should be included in the curriculum of the public schools declared that the state legislature not only had the power to decide what studies should be taught in the public schools of the state, but that it might also by statute give the local school authorities the right to determine this matter for their own school.

Indiana has several cases [21] in which the Supreme Court has recognized, either directly or indirectly, the power of the legislature to determine the composition of the curriculum of the common schools. The Supreme Court [2] in 1889 held that, as an incident of the principal power to establish, maintain, and control the public schools, the legislature also had the power to "prescribe the course of study." There are a number of jurisdictions [22] in agreement with this holding.

(2) *High School Courses*. The decisions [23] almost unanimously support the proposition that the legislature of a state has the power to require that a local school corporation shall furnish free high school education to all the youth of school age in the school district without distinction or discrimination. It is beyond the purpose of this study to go into a detailed investigation of the matter of school transfers. Nevertheless it may be stated here that the general rule of the decisions cited above is

to the effect that those school corporations that do not maintain such high school facilities are bound to transfer those of their pupils who desire to attend a high school to another school corporation and to pay the cost of such transfer, provided that the home corporation's trustees are consulted and their reasonable regulations followed.

Colorado has an interesting decision on this issue. The Colorado Supreme Court [24] in 1915 reversed the Colorado Appellate Court and held that a statute, which provided that a district that did not maintain a high school should pay the tuition of its pupils when attending high school in other districts, was unconstitutional. The ground upon which this decision was based was that the statute violated that provision of the state constitution which said that "said directors (of the local districts) shall have control of instruction in the public schools of their respective districts."

The Supreme Court of Ohio [25] in 1917 decided that, under the Ohio statute, a village district not maintaining a high school was not required to pay the tuition of its resident pupils when they attended high school elsewhere. It decreed:

Although each board of education is required by law to establish and maintain a sufficient number of elementary schools to provide for the free education of the youth of school age within the school district, the provisions of the statute with reference to the establishing of high schools is not mandatory.

The Requirement That Particular Things Be Taught

Dr. J. K. Flanders has recently published a study [32], *Legislative Control of the Elementary Curriculum*. This study revealed the extent to which the legislatures of the different states had made use of their power to prescribe the teaching of certain subjects, particular subject matter, and related items in the elementary public schools. The number of prescriptions represented in the statutes of the different states at three different dates, 1903, 1913, and 1923, was determined. Concerning the use of this authority, Dr. Flanders, on page 177 of his book, says:

Each of the forty-eight states is aware of its authority to legislate regarding the content of the elementary curriculum. To some extent every one of the states is exercising this authority and throughout the period covered by this study has exercised such authority. There is a wide variation in practice among the different states; some have enacted a long list of prescriptions, others very few; some have delegated large discretionary authority to the state board of education, others have left the control of the schools and of the curriculum almost entirely to local boards; in some states the voters of a district may prescribe additional subjects to the curriculum; some states have been reluctant to delegate any authority. There is no state where some discretion as to the subjects to be taught is not left to educational authorities and in every state there is abundant freedom to select the subdivisions which shall be included in a given subject. There is no single subject which, by direct mandate, is uniformly required throughout the common schools of the country.

Dr. Flanders, on page six of his book, makes this statement:

A high percentage of the approximately twenty-two hundred prescriptions embody some sort of unique or exceptional provision.

These twenty-two hundred prescriptions were classified by Dr. Flanders under sixty titles which he grouped under eight headings as follows: "Nationalism"; "Health and 'Prohibition' "; "Conservation of Life and Property"; "Practical and Cultural Subjects"; "Humaneness"; " 'Fundamental' Subjects"; "Religious and Ethical Subjects"; and "Miscellaneous Subjects."

It seems rather significant that in the present study the author has found cases involving this power of legislative prescription of the curriculum which fall only in the groups designated by Dr. Flanders as "Nationalism," "Practical and Cultural Subjects," and "Religious and Ethical Subjects." The cases found fall into Dr. Flanders' subclassifications as follows: Under "Nationalism": in the subdivisions denominated "Patriotism," "All Instruction in English," "Foreign Language," and "German"; under "Practical and Cultural Subjects": in the subdivisions denominated "Agriculture," "Music," "Household and Industrial Arts"; under "Religious and Ethical Subjects": in the subdivisions denominated "Sectarian Doctrine," and "Bible Reading." Cases involving the matter of the prescription of practical and cultural subjects have already been discussed, particularly in Chapter II. Cases involving religious and ethical subjects will be treated in Chapter V. Cases that have a connection with nationalism will be discussed at this point.

The Exclusion of Certain Things from the Curriculum

Foreign Languages. The question of the teaching of foreign languages in the states of the Union was not one that arose for the first time during the late World War. Certain precedents had been established by legislation and the attitude of the courts of many of the states on this question had been revealed through a long period of years. In 1874 the Michigan Supreme Court [26] had this issue before it and it held that, under the constitution and the statutes of Michigan, the local school officials might levy and collect a tax to support a school (high school) in which instruction was given in other languages than the English. In this case the Court took judicial notice of the historical facts connected with the adoption of the Michigan Constitution in 1850 and stated that the records showed that this very question had caused the wording of the constitution to be so changed that it might not prohibit the teaching of other languages than the English in the common schools.

In 1881 the Illinois Supreme Court [20] sustained the right of local school officials to prescribe the teaching of German or other foreign languages in their schools under the statute providing that such schools

shall be for the instruction in the branches of education . . . and such other branches, including music and drawing, as the directors, or the voters of the district at the annual election of directors, may prescribe.

This statute was held to be authorized by the constitutional provision that:

The general assembly shall provide a thorough and efficient system of free schools, whereby all the children of the state may receive a good common school education.

The Missouri Supreme Court [27] in 1883 held that since the legislature had committed the control of the city school fund to the city of St. Louis without any conditions, the city might teach whatever languages the school officials desired to have taught without any restriction by the courts.

The Kentucky Court of Appeals [28] in 1887 decided that the teaching of Latin and Greek in the common schools was a violation neither of the common-school law nor the constitution of the state or the nation.

In 1891 the Supreme Court of Indiana sustained a law [29] which provided that, upon the petition of the parents or guardians of twenty-five or more pupils of a school, the teaching of the German language as a branch of study should be required in any school of a township, town, or city. The Court held, furthermore, that the local officials of a city could not restrict this teaching of German to certain grades or certain buildings, but that it should be taught in all schools where the petition prevailed.

The Supreme Court of Kansas [30] in 1893 declared that a statute which provided that "the instruction given in the several branches taught shall be in the English language" was not violated by the mere fact that the Latin and German languages were taught, provided only that the medium of instruction must in all cases be the English language and not the foreign language that was the subject matter of instruction.

In 1916 the Supreme Court of Nebraska sustained a statute [31] under which a school city was providing instruction in such "modern European language" as the petition of the parents or guardians of fifty pupils above the fourth grade might request.

With the period of the World War came a great change in sentiment and this was reflected in the laws passed by the legislatures of several states [32]. The controversies resulting from the attempts to enforce these laws soon reached the higher courts and these cases are sometimes referred to as the "Language Cases." The most important cases dealing with the power and right of a state legislature to exclude the teaching of foreign languages from the schools of the state are those of the United States Supreme Court, decided in 1923 and carried up to the Supreme Court from the states of Nebraska, Iowa and Ohio. So far as the writer has been able to determine, this is the only instance in which the Supreme Court of the United States has passed upon the issue of the power and the right of a state to exclude the teaching of particular things from the schools of that state. For this reason these cases will be discussed somewhat in detail.

In 1919 the Nebraska Legislature passed "an act [33] relating to the teaching of foreign languages in the State of Nebraska." This act provided for a fine and imprisonment for its violation. The first two sections of the act read as follows:

Sec. 1. Instruction in foreign languages prohibited.—No person, individually or as a teacher, shall, in any private, denominational, parochial or public school, teach any subject to any person in any other language than the English language.

Sec. 2. Same, exception. Languages, other than the English language, may be taught as languages only after a pupil shall have attained and successfully passed the eighth grade as evidenced by a certificate of graduation issued by the county superintendent of the county in which the child resides.

The first case to be decided by the Supreme Court of Nebraska [34] under this statute was that of *Nebraska District of Evangelical Lutheran Synod of Missouri, Ohio and Other States, et al.* v. *McKelvie, Governor, et al.* The Synod asked for an injunction to restrain the State from enforcing this law. The Supreme Court by a divided stand refused the injunction and upheld the law in 1919. This case was not appealed to the United States Court.

In 1921 the Nebraska legislature passed an act intended to strengthen the act of 1919. The nature of this act [35] is shown by its title:

An act to declare the English language the official language of this state, and to require all official proceedings, records and publications to be in such language and all school branches to be taught in said language in public, private, denominational and parochial schools, etc.

The next one of these cases was that of *Meyer* v. *Nebraska* [36] which was decided by the Supreme Court by a divided stand in 1922 and appealed to the United States Supreme Court by Meyer as plaintiff in error. Meyer was convicted of a misdemeanor for violation of the act as quoted. Mr. Justice Mc-Reynolds of the United States Supreme Court [37] sums up the essential facts of this case in part as follows:

The Supreme Court of the State (Nebraska) affirmed the judgment of conviction. . . . It declared the offense charged and established was "the direct and intentional teaching of the German language as a distinct subject to a child who had not passed the eighth grade," in the parochial school maintained by Zion Evangelical Lutheran Congregation, a collection of Biblical stories being used therefor. And it held that the statute forbidding this did not conflict with the Fourteenth Amendment (Federal Constitution) but was a valid exercise of the police power.

It will help the reader to get a clear understanding of just what the issues of this case were to quote further from the decision of Justice McReynolds. He sets forth some things that were not at issue in this particular case but which are sometimes thought to have been decided by the case:

> The power of the State to compel attendance at some school and to make reasonable regulations for all schools, including a requirement that they shall give instructions in English, is not questioned. Nor has a challenge been made of the State's power to prescribe a curriculum for institutions which it supports. Those matters are not within the present controversy. Our concern is with the prohibition approved by the Supreme Court (of Nebraska).

Justice McReynolds makes a very clear statement of the issues that were actually before the Supreme Court of the United States as follows:

> The problem for our determination is whether the statute as construed and applied unreasonably infringes the liberty guaranteed to the plaintiff in error by the Fourteenth Amendment (to the U. S. Const.). . . . "No state shall . . . deprive any person of life, liberty, or property, without due process of law." . . .

When considering the issues as stated, this question at once arises. Just what does the term "liberty," as used in the Fourteenth Amendment, mean and what things does it include? On this point the Court says:

> While this court has not attempted to define with exactness the liberty thus guaranteed, the term has received much consideration and some of the included things have been definitely stated. Without doubt, it denotes not merely freedom from bodily restraint but also the right of the individual to contract, to engage in any of the common occupations of life, to acquire useful knowledge, to marry, to establish a home and bring up children, to worship God according to the dictates of his own conscience, and generally to enjoy those privileges long recognized at common law as essential to the orderly pursuit of happiness by free men.

Another question arises. May not the State, under the exercise of its police power, interfere with this liberty of its citizens? The answer, in terms of the Fourteenth Amendment, is that it may do so by "due process of law." What constitutes due process of law? Again the answer is available from the decision:

The established doctrine is that this liberty may not be interfered with, under the guise of protecting the public interest, by legislative action which is arbitrary or without reasonable relation to some purpose within the competency of the State to effect.

This question naturally follows. Has not the State legislature the power to determine what acts of its citizens are subject to restraint by its police power? The answer from the decision is:

Determination by the legislature of what constitutes proper exercise of the police power is not final or conclusive but is subject to supervision by the courts.

Another pertinent question emerges. Is the vocation of teaching German, as practiced by the plaintiff, such a vocation as individuals have the liberty of practicing under the law, or is the mere knowledge of a language other than English, on the part of children who have not passed the eighth grade, something which the police power of the State may properly prevent them from obtaining? On this point the Court says:

Mere knowledge of the German language cannot reasonably be regarded as harmful. Heretofore, it has been commonly looked upon as helpful and desirable. Plaintiff in error taught this language in school as part of his occupation. His right thus to teach and the right of parents to engage him so to instruct their children, we think, are within the liberty of the Amendment.

The Supreme Court of Nebraska had by this time held, in another case [38], involving the same parties as did the case in 1919, that the "so-called ancient or dead languages" are not "within the spirit or the purpose of the act" and that such languages as Latin, Greek, and Hebrew might be taught; but German, French, Spanish, Italian, and every other alien speech were banned. Justice McReynolds commented on this point as follows:

Evidently the legislature has attempted materially to interfere with the calling of modern language teachers, with the opportunities of pupils to acquire knowledge, and with the power of parents to control the education of their own.

May not the State make requirements of its citizens that are calculated to promote civic development and to foster American ideals through assuring that all children of tender years shall

be taught in the English tongue?   The following statement from
the decision covers this point:

> That the State may do much, go very far, indeed, in order to improve
> the quality of its citizens, physically, mentally, and morally, is clear;
> but the individual has certain fundamental rights which must be
> respected.   The protection of the Constitution extends to all, to those
> who speak other languages as well as to those born with English on
> the tongue.   Perhaps it would be highly advantageous if all had ready
> understanding of our ordinary speech, but this cannot be coerced by
> methods which conflict with the Constitution.—A desirable end cannot
> be promoted by prohibited means.

It is a matter of common knowledge that at the time of
the passage of such laws as the one upon which the conviction
of plaintiff in error, Meyer, was secured, owing to the feeling
incident to the Great War, many states passed laws of varying
degrees of severity and of similar nature to the Nebraska law.
Such was the case [32] in thirty-four of the states of the Union
in 1923.   Under our Federal constitution, may a state legislature
respond to popular feeling with such a law?   Justice McReynolds
discussed this question as follows:

> The desire of the legislature to foster a homogeneous people with
> American ideals prepared readily to understand current discussions
> of civic matters is easy to appreciate.   Unfortunate experiences during
> the late war and aversion toward every characteristic of truculent
> adversaries were certainly enough to quicken that aspiration.   But the
> means adopted, we think, exceed the limitations upon the power of
> the State and conflict with rights assured to plaintiff in error.   The
> interference is plain enough and no adequate reason therefor in time
> of peace and domestic tranquillity has been shown.

Perhaps someone will ask: "Was there not an emergency
sufficient to justify this law?   Were not certain citizens abusing
some of the rights guaranteed by the State and Federal constitutions?"   The answer is embodied in this decision:

> *Adams* v. *Tenner,* 244 U. S. 549, pointed out that mere abuse incident
> to an occupation ordinarily is not enough to justify its abolition, al-
> though regulation may be entirely proper.   No emergency has arisen
> which renders knowledge by a child of some language other than
> English so clearly harmful as to justify its inhibition with the conse-
> quent infringement of rights long freely enjoyed.   We are constrained

to conclude that the statute as applied is arbitrary and without reasonable relation to any end within the competency of the state.

The judgment of the Nebraska Supreme Court was reversed and the cause remanded for further proceedings not inconsistent with the opinion of the United States Supreme Court.

The United States Supreme Court on the same day that it decided the case of *Meyer* v. *Nebraska* also decided four other cases of a similar nature. The facts of these cases were such that the Court decided them upon the authority of the above case.

In *Bartels* v. *State of Iowa* [39] the plaintiff in error, Bartels, was convicted of teaching pupils below the eighth grade in a parochial school to read German contrary to "An Act requiring the use of the English language as the medium of instruction in all secular subjects in all schools within the state of Iowa, approved April 10, 1919." This teacher used English for teaching the common school branches, but taught young pupils to read German. The Supreme Court of Iowa was divided, three of the judges being in favor of sustaining the conviction and two in favor of reversing the decision of the lower court.

In the cases [40] of *Bohning* v. *State of Ohio* and *Pohl* v. *State of Ohio* the plaintiffs in error, Bohning and Pohl were severally convicted of violating a statute which prohibited the teaching of German to pupils below the eighth grade in any schools, public, parochial, or private, in the State. Bohning was an official and Pohl was a teacher in a parochial school in which German was taught to pupils below the eighth grade. The Supreme Court of Ohio was unanimous in affirming their conviction.

In the case of the *Nebraska District of Evangelical Lutheran Synod of Missouri, Ohio and Other States, et al.* v. *McKelvie, et al.*, decided in the Nebraska Supreme Court [38] in 1922, the Synod sought an injunction against McKelvie, Governor of Nebraska, to prevent the enforcement of "An Act to declare the English language the official language of this state, and to require all official proceedings, records and publications to be in such language and all school branches to be taught in said language in public, private, denominational and parochial schools," etc., approved in April, 1921. Although the Court was divided, the injunction was refused in the Nebraska Supreme Court and the case was appealed to the United States Supreme Court.

The Supreme Court of the United States reversed the four cases [41] just described, holding that they presented the same issues as did the case of *Meyer* v. *Nebraska* and deciding them upon the authority of that case. However, Justice Holmes delivered a dissenting opinion in which Justice Sutherland concurred. In presenting his dissenting opinion Justice Holmes said:

We agree, I take it, that it is desirable that all citizens of the United States should speak a common tongue, and therefore that the end aimed at by the statute is a lawful and proper one. The only question is whether the means adopted deprive teachers of the liberty secured to them by the Fourteenth Amendment. It is with hesitation and unwillingness that I differ from my brethren with regard to a law like this, but I cannot bring my mind to believe that in some circumstances, and circumstances existing, it is said, in Nebraska, the statute might not be regarded as a reasonable or even necessary method of reaching the desired result. The part of the Act with which we are concerned deals with the teaching of young children. Youth is the time when familiarity with a language is established and if there are sections in the state where a child would hear only Polish or French or German spoken at home, I am not prepared to say that it is unreasonable to provide that in his early years he shall hear and speak only English at school. But if it is reasonable, it is not an undue restriction of the liberty either of teacher or scholar. No one would doubt that a teacher might be forbidden to teach many things, and the only criterion of his liberty under the constitution that I can think of is "whether, considering the end in view, the statute passes the bounds of reason and assumes the character of a mere arbitrary fiat." . . . I think I appreciate the objections to the law but it appears to me to present a question upon which men reasonably might differ and therefore I am unable to say that the constitution of the United States prevents the experiment being tried. I agree with the court as to the special provisions against the German language contained in the statutes dealt with in *Bohning* v. *Ohio* decided today.

It is significant that the United States Supreme Court did not include the point of religious liberty in its discussion of the issues and in its decision of these cases. All the plaintiffs in error were representatives of denominational or parochial schools. The reports of the Iowa case and the Nebraska cases show that both the attorneys and the courts placed considerable stress upon the point, whether or not the statutes deprived these citizens of their religious liberty as liberty is guaranteed by the Fourteenth Amendment. The United States Supreme Court, in defining this liberty, merely referred to the right "to worship God according to the dictates of his own conscience" as one of the elements of such liberty. The pastor of the congregation in charge of the school involved in the case [37] of *Meyer* v. *Nebraska* testified as follows concerning the reason for teaching German:

. . . for instance, so that the children can take part in the devotional exercises of the parents at home, attend public worship with the parents and worship with them—for that reason we wanted to have the children learn so much German that they could be able to worship with their parents. That was the ultimate and only object we had in view in teaching German.

The exclusion of the Bible and religion from the public schools by the legislature will be dealt with in connection with the chapter on "Judicial Decisions Relating to Religion and the Bible in the Public Schools."

THE TREND OF THE DECISIONS

The general trend of the decisions of the state courts has been toward upholding and favoring increased and specific curricular prescriptions by the legislature. This general trend has the following divisions:

1. There has been a continuation of the trend favoring increased educational opportunities for children through the almost universal upholding of the legislature's power to require that the local school corporation shall furnish high school instruction in its own school or pay tuition for its pupils elsewhere.

2. There has been a trend toward upholding the legislature's power to make specific curricular prescriptions concerning what shall be taught to the children of school age in the state.

    a. There was a particular trend—up until the time of the adverse decision by the United States Supreme Court in 1923—toward upholding the legislature's power to exclude the teaching of foreign languages—particularly

German—to children below certain grades in schools other than public schools as well as in the public schools.

SUMMARY

I. The constitution of a state is not a grant of legislative power, but is a limitation upon it. Unless the constitution in express terms or by necessary implication limits the power of the legislature, it may exercise its discretion and adopt any measure which in its judgment will promote the efficiency of the schools and the cause of education in the state.

II. The following principles have been isolated by different courts when construing the legislature's duty and power to establish, maintain, and control "a uniform system of common or public schools."

1. Uniformity in executive administration must be provided.

2. The system need not be limited to the use of the so-called common or lower branches of study.

3. Uniform textbooks are not necessarily implied.

4. Similar officials should have similar powers.

III. Specific Controls by the State Legislature.

1. The legislature has the sole power to determine what system of education shall be used in the state.

2. The power of the legislature to prescribe courses of study or to require that particular things be included in the curriculum of the public schools has not been questioned by any of the decisions studied.

3. In every case studied the decision of the court has upheld the power of the legislature to require local school corporations to provide high school instruction for their pupils.

4. In every case except one the decision of the court has upheld the power of the legislature to require local school corporations to pay the cost of high school instruction incurred by their pupils elsewhere when the local school corporation did not maintain a high school.

5. The Colorado Supreme Court held in 1915 that the constitutional provision "said directors shall have con-

trol of instruction in the public schools of their respective districts" was violated by a statute requiring local school boards to transfer their high school pupils to some high school district when they did not maintain a high school.

6. The power of the legislature to prescribe courses of study or to require that particular things be included in the curriculum of schools other than the public schools has not been an issue for adjudication in any of the cases studied.

7. The power of the legislature to exclude certain things from the curriculum of the public schools has not been questioned in any of the decisions studied.

8. The power of the legislature to exclude foreign languages—particularly German—from the curriculum of schools other than the public schools was upheld by the Supreme Courts of Nebraska, Iowa, and Ohio, but upon appeal to the United States Supreme Court this exclusion was held to infringe unreasonably the liberty guaranteed by that section of the Fourteenth Amendment to the Constitution of the United States which provides that "No State shall . . . deprive any person of life, liberty, or property, without due process of law."

CITATIONS ON CHAPTER III

1. State v. Levitan, 181 Wis. 326.
2. State v. Haworth, 122 Ind. 462.
3. Fallett v. Sheldon, 144 N. E. (Ind.) 867.
4. Ehle v. State, 133 N. E. (Ind.) 748;
   School City v. Forrest, 168 Ind. 94;
   Stone v. Fritts, 169 Ind. 361.
5. Belles v. Burr, 76 Mich. 1.
6. Child Welfare v. Kennedy, 220 Mich. 296.
7. In Re Kindergarten Schools, 18 Colo. 234, a judicial opinion given at the request of the Legislature.
8. Alexander v. People, 7 Colo. 155;
   People v. Young, 309 Ill. 27;
   Piper v. Big Pine School Distr., 226 P. (Cal.) 926;
   In Re School Code 1919 (Opinion to State Legislature), 108 A. (Del.) 39;
   Smiddy v. City of Memphis, 203 S. W. (Tenn.) 512;
   Pronovost v. Brunette, 36 N. D. 288;
   Macmillan Co. v. Clarke, 184 Cal. 491.
9. Macmillan Co. v. Clarke, 184 Cal. 491.

10. Roach v. Board, 7 Mo. App. 567. In agreement are: Board v. Minor, 23
     Ohio St. 211; Benedict Schools v. Bradford, 111 Ga. 801; Board v.
     Purse, 101 Ga. 422; State v. Webber, 108 Ind. 31.
11. Campana v. Calderhead, 17 Mont. 548.
12. Ellis v. Greaves, 82 Miss. 36.
13. Barber v. Alexander, 120 Ga. 30.
14. Associated Schools v. School District, 122 Minn. 254.
15. Prowse v. Board, 134 Ky. 365.
16. Cusack v. Board, 79 N. Y. S. 803.
17. Cusack v. Board, 174 N. Y. S. 136.
18. Cusack v. Board, 85 N. Y. S. 991.
19. State v. Totten, 175 N. W. (N. D.) 563.
20. Powell v. Board, 97 Ill. 375.
21. State v. Webber, 108 Ind. 31;
     Fallett v. Sheldon, 144 N. E. (Ind.) 867;
     State v. Haworth, 122 Ind. 462.
22. State v. School District, 99 Neb. 338;
     Roach v. Board, 7 Mo. App. 567;
     Child Welfare v. Kennedy, 220 Mich. 296;
     State v. Totten, 175 N. W. (N. D.) 563;
     Powell v. Board, 97 Ill. 375;
     Fallett v. Sheldon, 144 N. E. (Ind.) 867;
     Bellmeyer v. Independent Distr., 44 Iowa 564;
     Epley v. Hall, 97 Kan. 549;
     Macmillan Co. v. Clarke, 184 Cal. 491;
     Campana v. Calderhead, 17 Mont. 548;
     Meyer v. State, 262 U. S. 390.
23. Taylor v. Matthews, 10 Ga. App. 852;
     People v. School Directors, 200 Ill. App. 250;
     Board v. School Directors, 201 Ill. App. 429;
     Board v. School Directors, 213 Ill. App. 91;
     People v. Moore, 240 Ill. 408;
     Cook v. Board, 266 Ill. 164;
     People v. School Directors, 267 Ill. 172;
     Swain v. Stewart, 267 Ill. 29;
     Board v. Haworth, 274 Ill. 538;
     Jeffersonville School Township v. School City, 50 Ind. App. 178;
     Independent District v. Solon, 162 Ia. 686;
     Independent District v. Carter, 168 Ia. 311;
     Hume v. Independent District, 164 N. W. (Ia.) 188;
     County Board v. Hopkinsville, 154 Ky. 309;
     Ricker Institute v. Inhabitants, 101 Me. 553;
     Associated Schools District v. School District, 122 Minn. 254;
     Independent District v. School District 12, 130 Minn. 19;
     Northern v. McCaw, 189 Mo. App. 362;
     New Hampton v. Northwood Distr., 74 N. H. 412;
     Lisbon Dist. v. Landaff Dist., 75 N. H. 324;
     Pushee v. Lyme Dist., 76 N. H. 369;

Board v. Grill, 133 N. Y. S. 394;
School Dist. v. School Dist., 40 Pa. Superior Court 311;
Wertz v. School Dist., 43 Pa. Sup. Ct. 1;
Grove v. School Dist., 43 Pa. Sup. Ct. 65;
School Dist. v. School Dist., 49 Pa. Sup. Ct. 561;
School Dist. v. School Dist., 50 Pa. Sup. Ct. 87;
Bensinger v. School Dist., 56 Pa. Sup. Ct. 226;
Board v. School Dist., 23 S. D. 429;
Town of Wallingford v. Town of Clarenden, 81 Vt. 245;
City of Columbus v. Town, 134 Wis. 593;
Free High School Dist. v. Town, 154 Wis. 564;
Finegan, Decisions N. Y. Supt., p. 276;
1 N. Y. S. Dep. Rep. 531;
10 N. Y. S. Dep. Rep. 449;
15 N. Y. S. Dep. Rep. 506;
20 N. Y. S. Dep. Rep. 170, 178, 180;
22 N. Y. S. Dep. Rep. 577;
23 N. Y. S. Dep. Rep. 441, 523;
24 N. Y. S. Dep. Rep. 691, 591;
26 N. Y. S. Dep. Rep. 46, 680;
27 N. Y. S. Dep. Rep. 285, 544, 605;
28 N. Y. S. Dep. Rep. 43, 457, 560, 710;
29 N. Y. S. Dep. Rep. 292, 326, 328, 335, 409, 459, 622;
30 N. Y. S. Dep. Rep. 136, 159, 162, 703, 706;
31 N. Y. S. Dep. Rep. 31, 170, 240, 243, 249, 251, 253, 455, 695, 718, 727;
32 N. Y. S. Dep. Rep. 80, 82, 177, 179, 182, 324, 533, 536, 602, 630, 705, 700;
33 N. Y. S. Dep. Rep. 5, 50, 58, 63, 73, 123, 334, 336, 338, 400, 509, 600.

24. School District v. High School, 60 Colo. 292;
25 Colo. App. 510.
25. State v. Bushnell, 116 N. E. (Ohio) 464.
26. Stewart v. School Dist., 30 Mich. 69.
27. Roach v. St. Louis, 77 Mo. 484.
28. Newman v. Thompson, 4 S. W. (Ky.) 341.
29. School Commr. v. State, 129 Ind. 14.
30. Board v. Welch, 51 Kan. 792.
31. Thayer v. School District, 99 Neb. 338.
32. Flanders, J. K., *Legislative Control of the Elementary Curriculum.*
33. Neb. Laws 1919, c. 249, p. 1.
34. Synod v. McKelvie, 104 Neb. 93.
35. Neb. Laws 1921, c. 61.
36. Meyer v. Nebraska, 107 Neb. 627.
37. Meyer v. State, 262 U. S. 390.
38. Nebraska Dist. of Evangelical . . . Synod . . . v. McKelvie, 108 Neb. 448.
39. Bartels v. State, 191 Ia. 1060.
40. Bohning v. State and Pohl v. State, 102 Ohio St. 474.
41. 262 U. S. 404.

CHAPTER IV

JUDICIAL DECISIONS RELATING TO THE CONTROL OF THE CURRICULUM OF THE PUBLIC COMMON SCHOOLS BY LOCAL AGENCIES

The decisions relating to the control of the curriculum by local agencies have been considered under two headings: control by parent and child and control by the local school corporation. While this classification of the decisions is not mutually exclusive at all points, it does serve to point the study toward the real parties in interest.

DECISIONS CONCERNING CONTROL BY PARENT AND CHILD

In order to understand the relation of the parent and the child to the control of the curriculum of the public schools it is necessary to go back to the relation that existed between the parent and the child at common law in regard to education. The Supreme Court of Georgia in 1897 stated this relation [1] as follows:

> At common law it was the duty of parents to give to their children "an education suitable to their station in life,—a duty pointed out by reason, and of far the greatest consequence of any" (1 Blackstone's Com. p. 450).

The Supreme Court of Oklahoma [2] in 1909 stated it after this fashion:

> At common law the parent, and especially the father, was vested with supreme control over the child, including its education, and, except when modified by statute, that authority still exists in the parent.

The Right of the Child to Instruction

Did the child have no rights in the matter of its education which it could enforce under the common law? The Court in the Georgia case, [1] referred to above, answered this question as follows:

The common-law rule being clear and unequivocal, that, while the duty rested upon the parent to educate his child, the law would not attempt to force him to discharge this duty, the child, so far as education is concerned, is completely at the mercy of the parent. Therefore, at common law the child had no right to demand an education at the hands of the parent.

How far may the state go in modifying this common-law rule? In answering this question the Indiana Supreme Court [3] in 1870 laid down this rule:

How far this interference should extend is a question, not of constitutional power for the courts, but of expediency and propriety, which is the sole province of the legislature to determine.

This same court [4] in 1901 took the following position:

The natural rights of a parent to the custody and control of his infant child are subordinate to the power of the state, and may be restricted and regulated by municipal laws. One of the most important natural duties of the parent is his obligation to educate his child, and this duty he owes, not to the child only, but to the commonwealth. If he neglects to perform it, or wilfully refuses to do so, he may be coerced by law to execute such civil obligation. The welfare of the child and the best interests of society require that the State shall exert its sovereign authority to secure to the child the opportunity to acquire an education.

Further light on the extent to which the legislatures of different states have restricted and modified the parent's right of control over the education of his child, in so far as it affects the curriculum of the common schools, will appear as a result of the discussion of some of the specific issues that have been raised by the attempts of parent and child to control the curriculum, as well as the acts of the state in extending the rights and opportunities of the child to obtain an education.

The Parent's Right to Select His Child's Studies versus *The Power of the Local School Authorities to Require Certain Studies*

The matter of the right of the parent to make for his child a selection from the studies offered in the curriculum clashes directly with the power of the local school corporation to require that the pupil take certain curricular provisions. It has been considered as less likely to lead to confusion of the reader, to discuss the cases involving these two rights under one heading.

The earliest case found, dealing with this issue, was decided in Vermont [5] in 1859. In this case the teacher had adopted a rule requiring the pupils to write compositions. A pupil refused to do so and was expelled. In this case the parent had not asked that the child be excused from writing compositions. The Supreme Court held that the rule was reasonable and upheld the action of the teacher in expelling the pupil.

The Supreme Court of Wisconsin had this question before it in 1874. The statute prescribed geography as one of the branches that should be taught in district schools. A father requested his boy not to study geography, desiring that he put more time upon his arithmetic. The teacher required that the boy study geography and upon his refusal to do so administered corporal punishment. The father claimed a parent's right to select the studies which his child should pursue. The Court held [6] that the teacher's action was unauthorized, saying in part:

> It is unreasonable to suppose that any scholar who attends school can or will study all the branches taught in them. From the nature of the case some choice must be made and some discretion be exercised as to the studies which the different pupils shall pursue. The parent is quite as likely to make a wise and judicious selection as the teacher. . . . It is impossible to say that the choice of studies which he made was unreasonable or inconsistent with the welfare and best interest of his offspring. . . . The statute gives the school board power to make all needful rules and regulations for the organization, graduation and government of the school, and power to suspend any pupil from the privileges of the school for non-compliance with the rules established . . . and it is not proposed to throw any obstacle in the way of the performance of these duties. But their powers and duties can well be fulfilled without denying to the parent all right to control the education of his children.

The Illinois Courts were called upon to rule upon this question three times between 1875 and 1878. In the first case [7], decided in 1875, the Supreme Court ruled that, where the local authorities had required that all the pupils in a certain class must take bookkeeping, a subject not prescribed by the statute, the teacher might not expel a pupil who refused to pursue this subject, acting upon the instructions of a parent.

In 1877 the Supreme Court [8] passed upon the same issue although it was raised in a different way. In an examination for entrance to high school a boy passed a satisfactory examination in all the studies except grammar, which the father did not desire him to study. The boy was refused admission. The Court held that the boy had a right to admission to all studies except grammar and that any rule excluding a pupil on that ground was unreasonable and could not be enforced. The position of the Court is shown by the following statement concerning the point in question.

But no attempt has hitherto been made in this state to deny, by law, all control by the parent over the education of his child. Upon the contrary, the policy of our law has ever been to recognize the right of the parent to determine to what extent his child shall be educated, during minority—presuming that his natural affections and superior opportunities of knowing the physical and mental capabilities and future prospects of his child will insure the adoption of that course which will most effectually promote the child's welfare. The policy of the school law is only to withdraw from the parent the right to select the branches to be studied by the child to the extent that the exercise of that right would interfere with the system of instruction prescribed for the school and its efficiency in imparting education to all entitled to share in its benefits.

In the third Illinois case a pupil attempted to maintain an action for damages against a teacher, basing his right of action upon the theory that there was an implied contract between a teacher and his pupil in the public schools to the effect that the teacher should hear the pupil recite. Acting upon an order of the local school directors, the teacher had refused to hear the pupil recite in any study unless he would first procure a copybook and take lessons in a certain system of penmanship. The Court [9] held that there was not such an implied contract and that the action could not be maintained.

The Ohio Supreme Court [10] in 1876 held that a rule of a local school board, which required that at stated times all pupils should be prepared to give some rhetorical exercise before the school, was a reasonable rule, enacted within the sound discretion of the board; that the pupil who was suspended for refusal to comply with this rule could not recover damages from the board.

A case which has been much criticized by other courts and which has been cited by the decisions as an example of the most extreme position which a court has assumed in upholding the right of the local school board to compel a pupil to take a prescribed subject is that decided by the Indiana Supreme Court [11] in 1886. A city superintendent expelled a high school boy for refusing, upon the direction of his father, to study music, as required by the local rules. The father would offer no excuse for not wanting his boy to study music but stood directly upon his right to exercise his choice. In supporting the local board the Court said in part:

It cannot be doubted, we think, that the legislature has given the trustees of the public school corporations the discretionary power to direct, from time to time, what branches of learning, in addition to those specified in the statute, shall be taught in the public schools of their respective corporations. We are of the opinion that the rule or regulation . . . was within the discretionary power conferred by law, . . . that it was not an unreasonable rule; but that it was such a one as each pupil of the high school, in the absence of sufficient excuse, might lawfully be required to obey and comply with.

The Nebraska Supreme Court has decided two cases of this character. In the one case [12], decided in 1891, the study to which the parent objected was grammar. His only reason for objecting was that "the study was not taught in the school as he had been instructed when he went to school." The Court upheld the right of the parent to make a selection of subjects and ruled that the local authorities must respect this right of the parent. No mention is made in this case of the reasonableness of the parent's action.

In the other Nebraska case [13], decided in 1914, the subject involved was that of domestic science. A father asked that his girl of 12 be excused from studying domestic science. He gave as his reasons the fact that to take this subject it was necessary that his daughter go to a different building, more than a mile distant from her regular school; that it took most of an afternoon, since the rules required that his child return at the end of the session to her regular school after the class in domestic science, merely for dismissal. He asked that she be allowed to come directly home from the domestic science class and this was refused. The Court's position is clear from the following quotation from the decision:

> The right of a parent to make a reasonable selection from the prescribed course of studies which shall be carried by his child in the free public schools of the state is not limited to any particular school, nor to any particular grade in any such public schools. School authorities are required to exercise their authority over and their desire to further the best interests of their scholars with a due regard to the natural and legal rights of the parents of such children.

The subject that caused the difficulty in Georgia was "composition and debate." A thirteen-year-old girl was assigned the topic "Should Trial by Jury be Abolished?" and required to write a composition which was to be read as a part of a debate. Her father objected, claiming (1) that he had a right to select the subjects which his daughter should take, (2) that the requirement was unreasonable, (3) that the exercise of debate was not a part of the prescribed course of the school. The Supreme Court [14] held that the authorities had power to require such an exercise; that whether the particular work assigned to the child was suited to her age and ability was a matter for the school authorities to determine and not for the courts; that a pupil might properly be expelled for refusal to comply with such a requirement.

In a case in Oklahoma, decided in 1909, the local authorities had required, in the absence of a statute specifically authorizing it, that children should take "all the studies in such course." After reviewing the cases and the authorities on this point the Supreme Court held [15] in part:

> The Oklahoma statutes have not entirely abandoned the common-law relations governing parent and child. . . . The right of the Board to prescribe the course of study and designate the textbooks to be used, does not carry with it the absolute power to require the pupils to study "all of the branches" prescribed in the course in opposition to the parent's reasonable wishes in relation to some of them.

It is important to note that the Court in this Oklahoma case stated that it could see no disaster to the schools in allowing the parent to select the course for his child.

A somewhat different phase of this question appeared in a case [16] decided by the Supreme Court of California in 1921. This Court held that, under a statute which gave the local school authorities the right and power to prescribe "courses in physical education," the local board had no power to determine, by resolution, that dancing, including round dances, is not opposed to religious scruples, and that all pupils must participate in such dancing as a part of the prescribed physical education course, contrary to the wishes of the parents of the pupils. The Court further declared that neither the state nor a school board has the right to enact a law or regulation which will, in effect and in a measure, alienate the children from parental authority so long as this aims to build up the personal character and advance the personal welfare of the children, and so long as the views of the parents are not detrimental to the moral well-being of the children nor inconsistent with the best interests of society.

Laws providing for the teaching of German, following the petition of patrons for such instruction, have been upheld in two states [17], Indiana and Nebraska. It is interesting to note that the matter of the teaching of German furnished the cause for the so-called Nebraska Language Cases discussed in Chapter III.

Right of the Parent to Have His Child Instructed Outside the Public Schools

The Indiana Appellate Court in 1903 held [18] that, under a statute which required that "every parent shall be required to send his child to a public, private or parochial school," it was sufficient compliance with the statute for a parent to procure a private teacher for his child, saying in part:

> The law was made for the parent who does not educate his child, and not for the parent who employs a teacher and pays him out of his private purse, and so places within the reach of the child the opportunity and means of acquiring an education equal to that attainable in the public schools of the state.

The Oklahoma Criminal Court of Appeals held [19] in substantial accord with the Indiana Court in 1922.

The Supreme Court of Washington decided [20] in 1912 that, under a statute which required that a parent send his child to a "public or private school," it was not a sufficient compliance that the parent, even though competent, instructed his child at home, since he did not in fact conduct a private school in his home.

The Supreme Court of Kansas in 1916 ruled [21] that, under a statute which provided that a parent must send his child to a public, private, denominational, or parochial school "for such period as said school is in session," the parent might not be prosecuted for taking his child out of the public school and sending him to a private school during the two months' session of such school.

The United States Courts have passed upon this question twice within recent years. The cases, known as the so-called Language Cases, carried up to the Supreme Court of the United States from the states of Nebraska, Iowa, and Ohio and decided there in 1923, have been discussed somewhat in detail in Chapter III under a subdivision of the topic, *Some Specific Controls by the State Legislature.* The discussion of those cases reveals the way in which the highest tribunal of the nation upheld the right of the parent to secure the instruction of his child outside the public school. It is not necessary to repeat that discussion here.

The Oregon Compulsory Education Amendment to the State Constitution provided that it should be a misdemeanor for any parent, guardian, or custodian of any child not excepted by the provisions of the Amendment and between the ages of 8 and 16 years, to fail to send such child to a public school. A private military school and a parochial school instituted suits [22] in the Federal District Court for the District of Oregon to have the Amendment declared void and to restrain its taking effect. The justice states the contentions of the plaintiffs thus:

Plaintiffs claim that the act is void as violative of section 1 of the 14th Amendment of the Constitution, in that it trenches upon their privileges and immunities as citizens of the United States; that it deprives them of life, liberty and property without due process of law, and the equal protection of the laws, and is violative also of that clause of section 10, article I of the constitution, relating to the impairment of the obligation of contracts.

Concerning the rights of parents under this situation the District Court said in part:

Further than this, a party insisting that constitutional guarantees for his benefit are being violated, may also insist, as an element of infringement of such guarantees, that others upon whom he is dependent for the support and sustenance of his lawful business shall not be deprived of their constitutional rights, privileges and immunities. . . .

To make the application here, the complainants in the instant cases have an interest in the parents and guardians of children of school age, and in the protection of their constitutional rights and liberties, and such parents and guardians have an interest in the constitutional rights of complainants to see that their schools may be maintained for the mutual use and benefit of the parties concerned. Thus the field of inquiry is broadened, and pertains, not only to whether the complainants' constitutional rights are affected adversely by the act in controversy, but to whether the constitutional rights of the parents and guardians are also adversely affected, for if they are so affected, complainants will be deprived, nevertheless, of the advantages of patrons with legal right and privilege of providing school attendance. . . .

It can scarcely be contended that complainants' rights to carry on their schools, whether parochial or private, is not a property right, and the right of parents and guardians to send their children and wards to such schools as they may desire, if not in conflict with lawful requirements, is a privilege they inherently are entitled to enjoy. . . .

The Child's Right to a Certificate of Having Completed a Curriculum

The Iowa Supreme Court is the only court which has been found to have had this issue before it. It has decided [23] two cases. In the first it was held in 1915 that the fact that a school board had allowed a pupil to participate in commencement exercises and to receive a "dummy" diploma did not entitle the pupil to a valid diploma when she had not made the required grades on her examinations. In the second case, decided in 1921, the Court held that a pupil who had met all the requirements for graduation, but who had refused to wear a "smelly" gown, provided for all graduates to wear at the commencement by the board, might later mandate the school officials to give her a diploma as a certificate of having completed the work of the required curriculum.

DECISIONS CONCERNING CONTROL BY THE LOCAL
SCHOOL CORPORATION

The Definition of the Term "Local" School Corporation

There may be some confusion as to the meaning of the term "local" when applied to a school corporation or school official. The Supreme Court of California [24] in 1880 explained the term as follows:

Each board, whether of a city, township or county, is "local" as to the territory of its jurisdiction. The board in a city is local as to the city; the board of a township is local as to the township, and the board of a county is local as to the county; and where portions of a county are subject to local boards for such portions, the County Board is local as to the balance of the county.

The Source of the Power to Control the Curriculum

It has already been shown in this study in Chapter III that the direct control of the schools, and the curriculum as well, is a function [25] of the legislature. Local school corporations are creatures of the legislature and the legislature by its statutes [26] determines the nature and extent of their power and control over the curriculum.

Concerning this control, the Michigan Supreme Court [27] in 1916 declared:

The general policy of the state has been to retain control of its school system, to be administered throughout the state under state laws by local state agencies organized with plenary powers independent of the local government with which, by location and geographical boundaries, they are necessarily closely associated and to a greater or lesser extent authorized to coöperate. In 99 Mich. 404 this court said, "Education belongs to the State. It is no part of the local self-government inherent in the township or municipality except so far as the Legislature may choose to make it."

The Minnesota Supreme Court [28] in 1919 when considering the status of local school governmental agencies under the constitution declared:

School districts are governmental agencies, wholly under the control of the Legislature, which may modify or abrogate their powers to any extent it sees fit.

The New York Commissioner of Education [29] in 1925 decided that the length of the school day was a matter within the discretion of the district trustee, under his general powers, subject to the supervisory control of the Commissioner and that he should exercise his discretion for the convenience of the majority of the parents and children.

The Indiana Supreme Court [30] as early as 1887 declared that a rule adopted by a board of education, which required that the city superintendent see that the best methods of instruction were adopted in the schools, necessarily conferred upon him authority, if he did not already have it, to order and promulgate such additional rules as the best interests of the schools might demand within the limits to which all such rules might extend.

The Missouri and Nebraska Supreme Courts [31] have decided that in the absence of the prescription of a course of study by the legislature the local school officials might prescribe a course under the general powers given them.

Since the legislatures of all the states have availed themselves of their power to prescribe a curriculum [32] the opportunity that is left to the local corporations is that of supplementing the curriculum prescribed by the state. No case has been found in the reports holding that the local corporation has original power to initiate and establish a curriculum.

The Kansas Supreme Court [33] in 1923 decided that, as between the local board and the annual meeting, where the statute made no designation of the seat of the power, the annual meeting could not by vote compel the board to maintain a full four-year high school course of study in order to provide college entrance credit for the local high school pupils who might later desire to go to college.

A Vermont town accepted a gift of money with which to purchase a building for a "graded school." It bought and equipped the building for school purposes, opened a school in it, and for two years raised taxes to operate the school. It also gave high school instruction for two years. The board then desired to avail itself of its right under the statute to pay the tuition of its high school pupils at another town's school. It was urged by the patrons that they had gained a vested right to the high school instruction and the high school in their own town. The Supreme

Court held [34] that this was not true; that the board might exercise its discretion as to its statutory right in this matter.

Rules and Regulations of the Local Corporation Controlling the Curriculum

(1) *In General.* There seems to be no doubt that the local school corporation's officials have the power to make all reasonable rules and regulations [35] for the government, discipline and management of the public schools. The Supreme Court of Indiana has stated [30] that "what are reasonable rules" is a question of law for the courts to decide. The Supreme Judicial Court [36] of Massachusetts in 1922 in interpreting the powers of the school committee of a Massachusetts city under the statute said:

> The school committee make all reasonable rules and regulations for the government, discipline and management of the schools under their charge. This includes a determination, within the bounds set by the statutes, of the subjects to be taught and the nature of the schools to be maintained and the exercise of discrimination, insight and wisdom in the election of teachers and in the general supervision of the school system, with all the incidental powers essential to the discharge of their main functions.

The local school corporations are created by the legislature for the express purpose of conducting the schools. No cases have been found in any state which denied the local corporations this general power of making reasonable rules and regulations. Naturally, questions which are most controversial are the ones that are most often carried to the higher courts. The matter of the use of the Bible and the various acts of a religious significance have given rise to many cases. These are deemed to be of such importance that they are discussed separately.

(2) *Extending the State's List of Prescribed Subjects.* If the legislature chooses to delegate to the local school corporation the power to extend the curriculum it is but exercising its power [37] to control the schools. Furthermore, it is but logical that, if this power be given or assumed by the local corporation, it must be exercised [38] in accord with the laws of the state in regard to such matters. In Chapter II of this study, which deals with "Judicial Decisions Relating to the Scope of the Cur-

riculum of the Public Common Schools," this power of the local school corporation to extend the state's list of prescribed subjects is necessarily shown as incidental to the main purpose of that discussion. The cases there discussed arose from the local school corporations' attempts to add subjects to their curricula that had not been specifically prescribed by the legislature. It is not necessary to repeat that discussion here, but it is important that the reader shall reread the chapter with the view of discovering the extent to which the local school corporations have been responsible for the addition of particular subjects to the curriculum and for the extension of the curriculum by the addition of the kindergarten and the high school. However, it is worthwhile to repeat that in the course of this study not a single case has been found in which the courts have denied the right of a local school corporation to add secular subjects to its curriculum, except where the legislature had made a specific prohibition, as in the case of the study of German.

(3) *Grading the Curriculum and Classifying Pupils.* If one is to judge by the number of cases found, there does not seem to have been much disposition to question the right of local school officials to grade the instruction presented in the schools and to classify the pupils accordingly. Cases have been found from seven states in which this issue has been decided. In all cases [39] the decisions held that the local school corporation had the right to grade and classify, and to enforce its decision.

The case decided by the Indiana Supreme Court seems to warrant special notice. In that case the statute provided that if a child had graduated from an elementary school under the age of sixteen the parent must send that child to high school. A parent attempted to avoid sending his child to high school by sending her to another elementary school. The Court held that by issuing a certificate of graduation the local school corporation had classified the pupil and that she must go to high school.

(4) *Denial of Part of the Curriculum to Certain Pupils.* Under this heading has been placed a case decided by the Supreme Court of Pennsylvania in 1913. In this case [40] it was sought, in defiance of a statute to the contrary, to exclude a boy from a special manual training school, which was maintained by the city, because he did not attend the public elementary school. It was contended that to permit this boy, who attended a sec-

tarian school during the day, to attend the special school maintained by the city would practically amount to giving the use of moneys raised for the public schools to private and sectarian schools. The Court decided that a child, otherwise eligible, could not be denied this part of the curriculum of the public schools.

Also under this heading has been placed those cases in which pupils have been denied the opportunity to participate in some of the so-called extra-curricular activities of the schools because they were members of high school secret societies. No attempt has been made in this study to take up the secret society question as it relates to the public schools in general. This is a subject for a special study. However, in a few cases local school boards have attempted to prevent the pupils of their schools from joining secret societies by passing rules that sought to deny to such secret society members the opportunity to represent the school in any way through participating in athletic, literary, military, and similar organizations or through participating in graduating exercises. These cases have been discussed because they do have a connection with the curriculum. In only one instance in the cases discussed has there been a statute covering the question. With that exception these cases involve only the board's powers to make general rules and regulations.

The Washington Supreme Court had this issue before it in 1906. Under a statute which authorized the school directors to adopt and enforce such regulations as might be deemed essential to the well-being of the school and to expel pupils who might refuse to obey the rules, the local school officials attempted to deny to pupils who belonged to a fraternity any participation in athletic, literary, military and similar activities. The Court held [41] that such action was within the authority of the local board, even though the meetings of the fraternity were held at the homes of the members, after school hours, and with the consent of the parents.

Illinois has two such cases. The first case was decided [42] by the Illinois Appellate Court in 1907 and upon appeal to the Supreme Court the decision [43] of the lower court was affirmed in 1908. In this case a rule of the superintendent of schools required that secret fraternities and sororities were to be denied all recognition by the teachers; that they were not to be permitted to meet in the school buildings; that such organizations were not to be allowed to use the name of the school; that no member of such societies should be permitted to represent the school in any athletic contest, literary contest, or in any public capacity. Although the rule stated that such societies were condemned, the members were not to be denied any of the regular school work and regular privileges. The Appellate Court held that such a rule was neither unlawful nor unjust. The Court said in part:

> The board and teachers stand *in loco parentis* to the pupils while attending school, and as a general proposition they are clothed with sufficient authority to determine what is and what is not for the best interests of the pupils intrusted to their care. Whenever such rules are not clearly so unreasonable as to be without the sanction of legal authority, they will be upheld by the courts. The presumption of law is in favor of the reasonableness of the rules of boards, like unto that of appellee's, and the burden of proving and maintaining that a rule is not reasonable rests on the party challenging it.

The decision of the Supreme Court in part follows:

> Assuming, as we must, that the adoption of the rule was not an abuse of power or discretion conferred by law upon the board, courts cannot, and should not, interfere with its enforcement. Pupils attending the schools may decide for themselves whether they prefer membership in the secret societies, with the disqualification from representing their schools in literary or athletic contests or other public capacities, or whether they prefer these latter privileges to membership in said societies. It is for the board of education, within the reasonable exercise of its power and discretion, to say what is best for the successful management and conduct of the schools, and not for the courts.

It may be of interest to note that a statute was passed in Illinois in 1919 making it unlawful for pupils in the public schools below the university and normal schools to belong to secret societies and rendering members of such societies liable to expulsion from the public schools. The Supreme Court upheld the constitutionality of this statute [44] in a decision rendered in a test case in 1923. Such statutes have also been upheld in several other states [45], as well as in the Federal Courts.

The one case of this kind that has been decided differently is that decided by the Missouri Supreme Court [46] in 1922. The rule of the school board in question in that case was substantially like that of the Illinois cases. The reason for the Missouri Court's decision is suggested in the opinion of the Supreme Court of Illinois in the case [44] in which it held the statute of Illinois against high school fraternities constitutional. The Court said in part:

In its opinion the Supreme Court (of Missouri) referred to the Wilson case (Illinois) and other cases, and said the powers of boards of education under the statutes of Missouri were more limited than they were in some other states, and the court refused to follow the decisions of other states on that question.

The Missouri Supreme Court [46] in discussing the authority of school boards generally in the adoption of rules of this character laid down this rule:

No rule should be adopted which attempts to control the conduct of pupils out of school hours after they have reached their homes, which does not clearly seek to regulate actions which, if permitted, will detrimentally interfere with the management and discipline of the school.

(5) *Control of Curricular Activities When Pupils Are Out of School.* The extent to which the local school authorities may go in making rules concerning practices which affect curricular activities, although the pupil be away from school when the act is performed, is defined somewhat by the following cases.

The New York Commissioner of Education in 1904 declared [47] that it was not only the right but the obligation of local school officials to exercise control over a newspaper that claimed to represent the high school, although it was not conducted at the school building.

The Texas Court of Appeals in 1887 held [48] that a rule which required that a pupil work two arithmetic problems outside of school was, under the provisions of the statute giving general powers of control to the local school authorities, a reasonable rule.

Under a statute which gave the local trustees power to prescribe rules for the government of the schools and power to suspend pupils for misconduct, the Mississippi Supreme Court in 1909 declared [49] that the local officials were without power to enforce a rule that pupils should remain in their homes and study between certain specified hours in the evening.

The Georgia Supreme Court in 1917 went so far as to hold [50] that a rule by the local school authorities against pupils attending picture shows on the nights of school days, except Friday, was a reasonable rule for the board to make as it tended toward the maintenance of good school work on the part of the pupils.

On the other side of this particular issue the Missouri Supreme Court in 1877 held [51] that a rule of a local board which forbade any pupil attending a social party was an invasion of the rights of the parent and so not enforceable.

The Iowa Supreme Court in 1906 decided [52] that, under a statute which authorized the local board to make rules and regulations for the government of pupils, the board might prohibit its pupils from playing football; that this power even extended to prohibiting the participation of pupils in a game which purported to be under the auspices of the school and by a team pretending to represent the school, although the game should be played outside school hours and neither on nor near the school grounds.

The right of a local board to make and enforce a rule that pupils should not leave the school grounds during school hours to receive instruction from unauthorized instructors, was sustained by the Supreme Court of Alabama [53] in 1924. The statute in Alabama gives such broad powers to the local school boards as "all the power necessary or proper for the administration and management of the free public schools."

(6) *Charging a Fee for Instruction.* One might think that there would be no question of fees for instruction arising in the higher courts of the United States where so-called free public schools have existed for so many years. However, there has been enough controversy over this issue to cause several cases to be carried to the higher courts. In 1891 the Georgia Supreme Court decided [54] that, under the constitutional provision that "public schools shall be free to all children," a public school, established under a local act, could not demand an "incidental fee" from resident students. In 1909 the same court decided [55] that a private school, operating a "common-school department" and receiving the common-school funds that would otherwise go to the maintenance of a common school by the

local board, could not exclude from such "common-school department" resident children who were otherwise qualified but who refused to pay a "matriculation fee."

Because the state constitution provided for a "free school system" the Supreme Court of Arkansas [56] in 1920 declared unconstitutional a special statute which sought to authorize a special school district to charge a fee for instruction at the discretion of the board.

The Kansas Supreme Court in 1904 made a similar decision [57] but it was based upon a constitutional provision which merely provided for a "uniform system of common schools and schools of a higher grade." It held that this provision implied that such schools should be free.

Alabama had, between 1910 and 1916, three Supreme Court decisions [58] which upheld a reasonable "incidental fee" of from ten to fifteen cents per pupil per month for the purpose of supplying fuel and light for the school house, since, at that time at least, there seemed to have been no statutory provision for a fund for heating and lighting school rooms. In one of these cases this Court forbade the charging of an incidental fee to supplement the teacher's salary.

The Kentucky Court of Appeals [59] in 1895, under a statute which declared that instruction should be free, upheld the right of local trustees to make a contract with a teacher in which it was provided that he might charge a fee for instructing pupils in studies which he was not required by law to teach, provided only that the efficiency of the work in the required subjects was not thereby impaired. The New York State Superintendent [60] in 1891, 1894, and 1896, ruled that the practice of allowing a teacher to teach subjects that are not required by law, such as stenography, typewriting, etc., and charge a fee therefor is illegal. His position was that any course that is given in a public school must be free. The Wisconsin Supreme Court [61] took a similar position with reference to charging a fee for manual training in 1910.

The Georgia Supreme Court [62] in 1905 decided that, although a statute gave a local school board the power to purchase textbooks and rent them to pupils, the board could not make the payment of such rent a condition precedent to a child's entering the schools when it already had such books.

The Supreme Court of South Carolina [63] in 1924 upheld a special statute which authorized the charging of a matriculation fee by the local trustees for the purpose of extending the term of school and paying the debt for a building.

(7) *Establishing Standards of Excellence in Work.* The power of a local board to exclude a pupil from high school because his grades did not come up to a particular standard of excellence established by the school officials was passed upon by the Supreme Judicial Court [64] of Massachusetts in 1913. The same case was again before the Court [64] in 1915. The pupil in question was given an opportunity to attend another school in the city, which was more adapted to his ability. The Court held that, under the statute giving the local board general control over the schools, such a rule was within its power.

An incidental phase of this question furnished the cause of action in a case decided by the Nebraska Supreme Court [65] in 1892. The Court decided that the local board of a high school had the power, under a statute which gave such boards power to adopt and enforce appropriate and reasonable rules for the government and management of the schools, to make a rule which required that the teacher keep a record of the standing of each pupil in his studies, attendance and deportment; that a written report of the same be sent to the parent each month; and that the parent be required to sign and return such report to the teacher.

(8) *Preventing Disloyal Instruction.* The New York Commissioner of Education [66] was called upon during the period of the World War to pass upon the matter of the local board's power to dismiss teachers who assumed an attitude in regard to the war and its prosecution which the board considered disloyal. The holding was to the effect that neither religious beliefs nor the principle of academic freedom would excuse a teacher's failure to perform her public duty or her refusal to support the government.

(9) *Using Pupils in Practice Teaching.* In 1914 the West Virginia Supreme Court [67] decided that a local board might permit the pupils of its schools to be used as subjects in practice teaching without invading their legal rights. The right of school authorities, under the statutes, to have students revise the work of a fellow student and to suspend a pupil who

remained away from class because her work was so revised was upheld by the Supreme Judicial Court [68] of Massachusetts in 1915.

THE TREND OF THE DECISIONS

In deciding issues not covered by specific constitutional or statutory provisions as well as issues growing out of uncertain constitutional or statutory provisions, the general trend of the courts has been toward according the local school authorities greater control over the curriculum and the parent and child less control.

The trend is noticeable in the following:

1. The construing of broader and more definite powers to the local school officials in making all necessary and reasonable rules and regulations for carrying out their duties.

2. The lessening of the parent's absolute and arbitrary right to determine what studies his child shall pursue.

SUMMARY

The weight of the decisions seems to justify the following conclusions:

I. The child now has an enforceable statutory right to an education.

II. As against the power of the local school authorities to re-quire studies not specifically prescribed by statute, the parent still has the right to a reasonable selection from the studies offered.

III. The parent has the inherent and constitutional right to have his child instructed in a private, denominational, or parochial school, provided such schools meet the lawful requirements set up by statute.

IV. A. In general, the decisions hold that local school corporations are invested by the constitution and the legislature with sufficient power to make all reasonable rules and regulations necessary to carry out the obligations and duties laid upon them by the state, and also, with all incidental powers essential to the discharge of their main functions.

B. More specifically, the local school authorities may exercise the following controls over the curriculum:

1. They may add any secular subject to their curriculum, provided it is not proscribed by the legislature, or the constitution.

2. They have full power to grade the curriculum and classify their pupils, subject to statutory provisions.

3. They stand *in loco parentis* to the pupils and may, by a reasonable rule, deny a part of the curriculum to certain pupils if in their discretion it seems for the best interests of the pupils and the school as a whole.

4. They may adopt rules which seek to control the conduct of pupils out of school hours after they have reached their homes, provided, that the rules clearly seek to regulate actions which, if permitted, will detrimentally interfere with the work, management, and discipline of the school.

5. Generally speaking, they may not adopt rules which exact a fee for instruction.

6. They may adopt rules establishing standards of excellence in work.

7. They may use their pupils in practice teaching.

8. The New York Commissioner of Education has held that disloyal instruction may be prevented by the local officials.

CITATIONS ON CHAPTER IV

1. Board of Education v. Purse, 101 Ga. 422.
2. School Board v. Thompson, 103 Pac. (Okla.) 578.
3. State v. Clottu, 33 Ind. 409.
4. State v. Bailey, 157 Ind. 324.
5. Lander v. Seever, 32 Vt. 224.
6. Morrow v. Wood, 35 Wis. 59.
7. Rulison v. Post, 79 Ill. 567.
8. Trustees v. People, 87 Ill. 303.
9. Stuckey v. Churchman . . ., 2 Ill. App. 584.
10. Sewell v. Board, 29 Ohio St. 89.
11. State v. Webber, 108 Ind. 31.
12. Sheibley v. School District, 31 Neb. 552.
13. State v. Ferguson, 95 Neb. 63.
14. Bradford v. School, 111 Ga. 801.
15. School Board v. Thompson, 24 Okla. 1.
16. Hardwick v. Board, 205 Pac. (Cal.) 49.
17. Board of Commissioners v. State, 129 Ind. 14; State v. School District, 99 Neb. 338.

18. State v. Peterman, 32 Ind. App. 665.
19. Wright v. State, 209 Pac. (Okla.) 179.
20. State v. Cournort, 69 Wash. 361.
21. State v. Will, 99 Kan. 167.
22. Hill Military Academy v. Pierce et al., 296 F. 928;
    Society of Sisters, etc., v. Pierce et al., 296 F. 928.
23. Sweitzer v. Firlen, 172 Ia. 266;
    Valentine v. School Dist., 183 N. W. (Ia.) 434.
24. People v. Board of Education, 55 Cal. 331.
25. In addition to the discussion in Chapter III and the cases cited therein
    the following cases support this position:
    Thompson v. Elmo Independent Dist., 269 S. W. (Tex.) 868 (1925);
    State v. Milquet, 192 N. W. (Wis.) 392 (1923);
    Kuykendall v. Hughey, 224 Ill. App. 550 (1922);
    Macmillan v. Johnson, U. S. District Court, 269 F. 31 (1920);
    Watson v. City, 157 Mass. 561;
    Robinson v. Schenck, 102 Ind. 307.
26. In addition to the discussion in Chapter III see:
    Thompson v. Elmo Independent Dist., 269 S. W. (Tex.) 868 (1925);
    Ehle v. State, 133 N. E. (Ind.) 748 (1922);
    Thayer v. District, 99 Neb. 338;
    Fertich v. Michener, 111 Ind. 472.
27. MacQueen v. City Commissioners, 194 Mich. 328.
28. Kramer v. Renville County, 175 N. W. (Minn.) 101;
    Wilkerson v. Rome, 152 Ga. 762.
29. 33 New York State Department Reports 226.
30. Fertich v. Michener, 111 Ind. 472.
31. State v. Millsap, 130 Mo. App. 683;
    Sheibley v. School, 31 Neb. 552.
32. Flanders. *Legislative Control of the Curriculum,* p. 177.
33. State v. School District, 112 Kan. 66.
34. Samson v. Town Grand Isle, 78 Vt. 383.
35. Barnard v. Shelbourne, 216 Mass. 22;
    Board v. Minor, 23 Ohio St. 211;
    Donahue v. Richards, 38 Me. 378;
    Hodgkins v. Rockport, 105 Mass. 475;
    Downer v. Lent, 6 Cal. 94;
    Hines v. Lockport, 50 N. Y. 236;
    Jordon v. Hanson, 49 N. H. 199;
    Gregory v. Burke, 37 Conn. 365;
    Kendall v. Stokes, 3 How. (U. S.) 87;
    Roberts v. City, 59 Mass. 198;
    Sewell v. Board, 29 Ohio St. 89;
    Morrow v. Wood, 35 Wis. 59.
36. Leonard v. School Committee, 135 N. E. (Mass.) 459.
37. Donahue v. Richards, 38 Me. 379;
    State v. Haworth, 122 Ind. 462.
38. Indianapolis v. State, 129 Ind. 14.

39. State v. Board, 81 W. Va. 353;
    Westland Pub. Co. v. Royal, 36 Wash. 399;
    Trustees v. People, 87 Ill. 303;
    State v. School District, 31 Neb. 552;
    Finegan, Decisions N. Y. Supt. 185;
    Bd. of Ed. v. State, 80 Ohio St. 133;
    134 N. E. (Ind.) 209.
40. Commonwealth v. School Dist., 241 Pa. St. 224.
41. Wayland v. School Dist., 43 Wash. 441.
42. Wilson v. Board, 137 Ill. App. 187.
43. Wilson v. Board, 233 Ill. 464.
44. Sutton v. Board, 306 Ill. 517.
45. Bradford v. Board, 18 Cal. App. 19;
    University v. Waugh, 105 Miss. 623;
    Waugh v. Board, 237 U. S. 589;
    Lee v. Hoffman, 182 Iowa 1216.
46. Wright v. Board, 246 S. W. (Mo.) 43.
47. Finegan, Dec. N. Y. Supt. 94.
48. Hutton v. State, 23 Tex. App. 386.
49. Hobbs v. Germany, 94 Miss. 469.
50. Magnum v. Keith, 147 Ga. 603.
51. Dritt v. Snodgrass, 66 Mo. 286.
52. Kinzer v. Independent Dist., 129 Ia. 441.
53. Christian v. Jones, 100 S. (Ala.) 99.
54. Irwin v. Gregory, 86 Ga. 605.
55. Wilson v. Stanford, 133 Ga. 483.
56. Special School District v. Bangs, 221 S. W. (Ark.) 1060.
57. Board v. Dick, 70 Kan. 434.
58. Bryant v. Whisenant, 167 Ala. 325;
    Ryan v. Sawyer, 195 Ala. 69;
    Hughes v. Outlaw, 73 S. (Ala.) 16.
59. Major v. Cayce, 98 Ky. 357.
60. Finegan, Dec. N. Y. Supt., pp. 1305, 1315, 1330.
61. Maxcy v. City, 144 Wis. 238.
62. Mathis v. Gordy, 119 Ga. 817.
63. Felder v. Johnson, 127 S. C. 215.
64. Barnard v. Inhabitants Shelbourne, 216 Mass. 19, and 222 Mass. 76.
65. Bourne v. State, 35 Neb. 1.
66. 18 N. Y. St. Dept. Rep. 393;
    21 N. Y. St. Dept. Rep. 270 and 489;
    33 N. Y. St. Dept. Rep. 261.
67. Spedder v. Board, 74 W. Va. 181.
68. Wulff v. Inhabitants Wakefield, 221 Mass. 427.

CHAPTER V

JUDICIAL DECISIONS RELATING TO RELIGION AND THE BIBLE IN THE PUBLIC SCHOOLS

ANALYSIS OF DECISIONS BY STATES

Bible reading, prayers, hymn singing, the wearing of religious garb, and the use of sectarian and denominational buildings by public schools are some of the manifestations of man's religious impulses that have had a place in some of our public schools. These practices have been considered to be a part of the curriculum, a source of instruction. They have caused many controversies to be carried to the higher courts for final adjudication. It has been considered impractical to attempt to deal with these practices singly in presenting data. They have rarely occurred that way. They have involved the construction of the state constitution in all cases. Constitutions differ greatly. For these reasons the data for this chapter have been presented under state headings. A detailed analysis has been made of at least one case from every state in which the matter has been carried to the higher courts for adjudication. If other cases have occurred they are discussed without detailed analysis.

CALIFORNIA

Evans v. *Selma High School District, 222 P. (Cal.) 801, (1924)*

State Constitutional Provisions Cited:

Art. I, Sec. 4: The free exercise and enjoyment of religious profession and worship, without discrimination or preference, shall forever be guaranteed in this state; and no person shall be rendered incompetent to be a witness or a juror on account of his opinions on matters of religious belief; but the liberty of conscience hereby secured shall not be so construed as to excuse acts of licentiousness, or justify practices inconsistent with the peace or safety of the state.

Art. IV, Sec. 30 prohibits appropriations, grants, or payments of public moneys in aid of any religious sect, church, creed, or sectarian purpose, or to support or sustain any school or other institution controlled by any religious creed, church, or sectarian denomination whatever.

Art. IX, Sec. 8: No public money shall ever be appropriated for the support of any sectarian or denominational school, or any school not under the exclusive control of the officers of the public schools; nor shall any sectarian or denominational doctrine be taught, or instruction thereon permitted, directly or indirectly, in any of the common schools of the state.

Statutory Provisions Cited: The Political Code, section 1607, subdivision 3, makes it the duty of boards of education and school trustees:

. . . to exclude from school and school libraries all books, publications or papers of a sectarian, partisan, or denominational character.

Section 1672 of the same code provides that:

No publication of a sectarian, partisan, or denominational character may be used or distributed in any school, or be made a part of any school library; nor must any sectarian or denominational doctrine be taught therein.

Complainants: Patrons who are probably Catholic sympathizers.

Cause for Complaint: A local school board adopted a resolution authorizing the purchase of 12 copies of the King James version of the Bible for the library of the public high school.

Issues Involved: 1. Is the King James version of the Bible a book of a "sectarian, partisan, or denominational character"? 2. Does the purchase and placement in the high school library of the King James Bible constitute a violation of the constitution and the statutes of California?

Pertinent Factors: This is the first time that the general issue of sectarian influence has been raised by the matter of placing the Bible in a public school library.

Holding of the Supreme Court: By a unanimous decision the Court held: 1. That the King James version of the Bible is not a sectarian book. 2. Neither the constitution nor the statutes would be violated by placing any version of the Bible in a public school library. The Court said in part:

We are not required in this case to decide, nor are we to be understood as deciding, the question of whether or not the use of the Bible for class instruction amounts to the teaching of sectarian or denominational doctrine, nor to consider whether or to what extent its reading may be made a part of the exercises in the schools, without offending the provisions of the state Constitution and statutes. . . . We have examined with care all decisions cited by counsel and all that our independent research has discovered, and not one of them deals with the precise question now under consideration, namely, the placing of the Bible in a public school library. . . .

. . . The statute, however, deals with publications of a sectarian character. It makes the character of the book the test of whether it is "sectarian," not the authorship or the extent of its approval by different sects or by all. That the authors of religious books belong to a sect or church does not necessarily make their books of a sectarian character. Nor does the fact that the King James version is commonly used by Protestant churches and not by Catholics make its character sectarian. Its character is what it is, a widely accepted translation of the Bible. What we have said of the King James translation is equally applicable to the Douai version. Both are scholarly translations of the Bible, and neither is a book "of a sectarian character" within the meaning of the statute relating to school libraries. Both are eligible to a place on the shelves of our public school libraries for reference purposes.

Hardwick v. *School Board, 205 P. (Cal.) 49, (1921)*

This decision involves the right of liberty of conscience and religious freedom. In 1921 the California Supreme Court held that a school board had no power to declare that the teaching of dancing and the dancing itself, as a part of the physical education curriculum, was not opposed to the religious scruples or belief of any person or persons; furthermore, that the board had no power to exclude from school pupils who refused, upon instructions from their parents, to take part in such dancing. The Court held that such action by a school board would violate Article I, section 4, of the California constitution and that part of Amendment I of the constitution of the United States which provides that "Congress shall make no law respecting the establishment of religion, or prohibiting the free exercise thereof." The Court said in part:

The question involved in this controversy, however, is not necessarily one of religion or whether the dances mentioned in the complaint, and to which the appellant is opposed, are disapproved by the religious organization to which he belongs, if, indeed, he is a member of any such organization. It is as much a question of morals, which may concern the consciences of those who are not affiliated with any particular religious sect as well as those who are active members of religious organizations opposed to that form of amusement or exercise.

GEORGIA

Wilkerson v. City of Rome, 152 Ga. 762 (1922)

Provisions of State Constitution Cited:

Art. I, Sec. 1, Par. 12: All men have the natural and inalienable right to worship God, each according to the dictates of his own conscience, and no human authority should in any case control or interfere with such right of conscience.

Sec. 13: No inhabitant of this state shall be molested in person or property, or prohibited from holding any public office or trust, on account of his religious opinions, but the right of liberty of conscience shall not be so construed as to excuse acts of licentiousness, or justify practices inconsistent with the peace and safety of the state.

Sec. 14: No money shall be taken from the public treasury, directly or indirectly, in aid of any church, sect or denomination of religionists, or of any sectarian institution.

Complainants: Patrons who were probably Protestant sympathizers.

Cause for Complaint: The school board refused to enforce a city ordinance requiring that the principals provide for daily reading of the King James version of the Bible and prayer in the public schools.

Issues Involved: 1. Does the ordinance violate the state constitution? 2. Does Bible reading and prayer in public school violate the right of conscience of pupils? 3. Do such acts result in taking money from the public treasury in aid of "any sectarian purpose"?

Pertinent Factors: 1. Reading of Bible is to be without comment. 2. Pupils may be exempted from attending exercises upon request of parent.

Holding of the Supreme Court: By a divided decision the mandamus requiring the school board to enforce the ordinance was upheld, since the ordinance did not violate either of the clauses of the constitution. The Court in explaining its decision said in part:

It will conduce to a clearer construction by tracing to their origin the paragraphs of the constitution referred to, and ascertaining the evils intended to be cured by them. . . . There is abundant historical evidence, as well as the opinions of eminent statesmen and jurists for the statement that the pioneers in the formation and conduct of American colonial governments did not have it in mind to bring about a complete separation of Church and State.

As stated in 10 Michigan Law Review, 164, "It is doubtful if in a single one of the colonies before the Revolution, there was absolute freedom of belief and worship. Thus in every one of the American colonies the State already endeavored to interfere in matters religious, and in most of them a State Church was established. Georgia was no exception to that rule. In Georgia in 1758 the Minister of Savannah (Episcopal) . . . was incorporated and made a body politic and corporate . . . enabled to sue and be sued and levy and collect taxes on all inhabitants for the support of the parish church. Apparently it was intended to engraft the Church of England upon the province." It should be clearly understood, however, that (this movement for the separation of Church and State) was not a movement for the separation of State from Christianity, but specifically, a separation of Church and State. Many statesmen treated Christianity as a part of the law of the land.

From an examination of all the constitutions of Georgia and of their origin, we think it clearly appears that the framers of our constitutions have never intended to declare the policy of this State to be unreligious or unchristian. They did intend, in the constitution of 1877, to prohibit taxation for the support of any church, denomination, or sectarian institution maintained as a State institution. Indeed the protection afforded by the constitution is a protection to individuals and not to Churches.

A quotation from the dissenting opinion reads:

This ordinance established a system of worship for the schools of Rome, and thus in this case controls or interferes with the individual worship of God. . . . Religious freedom includes the right not to worship God at all. . . . The exemption of certain classes from the operation of an unconstitutional enactment will not save its face.

The reading of this version (King James) offends and molests the Catholics and Jews. The reading of certain texts of this version will molest certain sects of Protestants. The system of worship provided for in this ordinance will offend the deists, atheists, and agnostics.

We cannot disguise the fact that making the reading of the King James version of the Bible a part of the worship of the public schools puts municipal approval upon that version, and thus discriminates in favor of and aids the Protestant sects of the Christian religion. . . . No public funds can be lawfully taken from the public treasury and used in any manner which aids any sect or denomination.

ILLINOIS

People v. *Board of Education, 245 Ill. 334, (1910)*

State Constitutional Provisions Cited:

Art. 2, Sec. 3: . . . No person shall be required to attend or support any ministry or place of worship against his consent; . . . the free exercise and enjoyment of religious profession and worship, without discrimination, shall not be abridged.

Art. 8, Sec. 3: Neither the General Assembly, nor any county, city, town, township, school district or other public corporation, shall ever make any appropriation, or pay from any public fund whatever, anything in aid of any church or sectarian purpose, or to help support or sustain any school, academy, seminary, college, university, or other literary or scientific institution, controlled by any church or sectarian denomination whatever, nor shall any grant or donation of land, money or other property, ever be made by the state, or any such public corporation, to any church or for any sectarian purpose.

Complainants: Patrons who are Catholics.

Cause for Complaint: 1. Reading of the King James Bible and commenting thereon.   2. Reciting of Lord's Prayer.   3. Hymn singing.

Issues Involved: 1. Did the exercises constitute a violation of the guaranty of freedom of worship?   2. Did the reading of the King James Bible constitute sectarian instruction?   3. Did the exercises result in the appropriation of public funds in aid of sectarian instruction or purposes?

Pertinent Factors: 1. Pupils were required to stand and assume a devotional attitude during the exercises.   2. Pupils were at times asked to explain Bible passages.

Holding of the Supreme Court: The Court by a divided decision answered the three questions at issue in the affirmative and reversed the decision of the lower court which had denied the petition for mandamus against the practices.   The Justice who wrote the majority opinion said in part:

The exercises mentioned in the petition constitute worship. They are the ordinary forms of worship usually practiced by Protestant

Christian denominations. Their compulsory performance would be a violation of the constitutional guaranty of the free exercise and enjoyment of religious profession and worship. One does not enjoy the free exercise of religious worship who is compelled to join in any form of religious worship.

The public schools are supported by taxation, and if sectarian instruction should be permitted in them the money used in their support would be used in aid of a sectarian purpose. The prohibition of such use of public funds is therefore a prohibition of the giving of sectarian instruction in the public schools. The reading of the Bible in school is instruction. Religious instruction is the object of such reading, but whether it is or not, religious instruction is accomplished by it. . . .

The only means of preventing sectarian instruction in the school is to exclude altogether religious instruction, by means of the reading of the Bible or otherwise. The Bible is not read in the public schools as mere literature or mere history. It cannot be separated from its character as an inspired book of religion. It is not adapted for use as a textbook for the teaching alone of reading, of history, of literature, without regard to its religious character.

A quotation from the dissenting opinion reads:

The Bible is not mentioned in the Constitution, nor is there found therein any express inhibition against the giving of religious or moral instruction in the public schools, and while the Constitution is silent upon these subjects, it has been from the formation of our state government to the present time universally recognized by the people that there are certain fundamental principles of religion and morality which the safety of society requires should be imparted to the youth of the state, and that those principles may be properly taught in the public schools as a part of the secular knowledge which it is their province to instill into the youthful mind.

McCormack v. Burt, 95 Ill. 263, (1880)

Illinois has one case involving the question of religious influence in the public schools in which the decision of the case was made on a more or less technical point of pleading. The controversy arose over the expulsion of a Catholic boy who refused to obey a rule of the school board to the effect that, during the opening exercises of the school and the reading of the King James Bible, all pupils should lay aside their books and remain quiet. The Supreme Court held that the attorneys for the expelled boy had made a fatal defect in their pleading when they failed to aver that the school directors had acted either wantonly or maliciously, seeing that the statute invested them with discretion in making rules for the school. The Court affirmed the decision of the lower court in favor of the school officials but did not decide the question of the legality of the Bible reading.

Millard v. *Board of Education, 121 Ill. 29, (1887)*

In this case the local school board rented a basement room in a Catholic church in which to hold the public school, claiming an emergency. The teacher was a Catholic. Some pupils voluntarily attended mass in the church and also voluntarily studied the catechism before the public school session started. The Angelus prayer was said at dismissal at noon. The complainant asked an injunction against holding the school in that place. The Supreme Court affirmed the decision of the lower court for the defendant, holding under the facts in the case that there was no ground for an injunction since it did not appear that the plaintiff's children were required against his wishes to attend or receive any religious instruction.

IOWA

Moore v. *Monroe, 64 Ia. 367, (1884)*

State Constitutional Provisions Cited:

Art. I, Sec. 3: The General Assembly shall make no law respecting an establishment of religion, or prohibiting the free exercise thereof; nor shall any person be compelled to attend any place of worship, pay tithes, taxes, or other rates for building or repairing places of worship, or the maintenance of any minister or ministery.

Statutory Provisions Cited:

Sec. 1764: The Bible shall not be excluded from any school or institution in this state, nor shall any pupil be required to read it contrary to the wishes of his parent or guardian.

Complainant: Patron of school. No evidence as to religious belief.

Cause for Complaint: Bible reading, Lord's Prayer, hymns in public school.

Issues Involved: 1. Constitutionality of Sec. 1764, Iowa Code. 2. Did the exercises make the schoolhouse a "place of worship?" 3. Were children compelled to "attend a place of worship?" 4. Was complainant compelled "to pay taxes for building or repairing a place of worship?"

Pertinent Factors: 1. Children were not required to be present at exercises.

Holding of the Supreme Court: 1. By unanimous decision the statute was held not unconstitutional. 2. The injunction asked against the exercises by the complainant was denied. The Supreme Court said in part:

We can conceive that exercises like those described might be adopted with other views than those of worship, and possibly they are in the case at bar; but it is hardly to be presumed that this is wholly so. For the purposes of this opinion it may be conceded that the teachers do not intend to wholly exclude the idea of worship. It would follow from such concession that the schoolhouse is, in some sense, for the time being, made a place of worship. But it seems to us that if we should hold that it is made a place of worship, within the meaning of the constitution, we should put a very strained construction upon it. The object of the provision, we think, is not to prevent the casual use of a public building as a place for offering prayer, or doing other acts of religious worship, but to prevent the enactment of a law whereby any person can be compelled to pay taxes for the building or repairing of any place designed to be used distinctively as a place of worship. The object, we think, was to prevent any improper burden. . . . Under this provision (Statute Sec. 1764), it is a matter of individual option with school teachers as to whether they will use the Bible in school or not, such option being restricted only by the provision that no pupil shall be required to read it contrary to the wishes of his parent or guardian.

Knowlton v. *Baumhover, 182 Iowa 691, (1918)*

Complainant: A patron, probably a Protestant sympathizer.

Cause for Complaint: The holding of a public school in a room of a Catholic parochial school.

Issues Involved: 1. Was there an appropriation of public funds for sectarian purposes within the meaning of Section 593 of the Iowa Code of 1897 which forbids the "use or appropriation or gift or loan of public funds to any institution or school under ecclesiastical or sectarian management or control?" 2. Was the school sectarian?

Pertinent Factors: 1. The public school building had been sold and a room in a Catholic parochial school rented for $2.50 per year. 2. A sister in religious garb was the teacher. 3. There were the usual furniture and decorations of a Catholic school. 4. This so-called public school was in reality only the upper grade department of the parochial school. 5. The teacher was paid by public funds.

Holding of the Supreme Court: In a unanimous decision the Court held that this school was sectarian and that public money was being appropriated for sectarian purposes in its support. Mandamus was ordered against the practices. The Court said in part:

It is the fixed policy of this nation and of its several states, to maintain the common school system free from sectarian influence or control, and to preserve the equal right of every citizen to have his children educated in the common schools of the people, without being subjected to the slightest sectarian leading on the part of their teachers. . . . If the plaintiff had done no more than to show that the reading of the Bible, in any version, or the use of the Lord's Prayer was practiced in this school his complaint would, of course, be dismissed.

KANSAS

Billard v. Board of Education, 69 Kan. 53, (1904)

State Constitutional Provisions Cited:

Art. 6, No. 7: The right to worship God according to the dictates of conscience shall never be infringed; nor shall any person be compelled to attend or support any form of worship; nor shall any control of or interference with the rights of conscience be permitted. . . .

Art. 6, No. 8: No religious sect or sects shall ever control any part of the common-school or university funds of the state.

Statutory Provisions Cited:

General Statutes 1901, Sec. 6284: No sectarian or religious doctrine shall be taught or inculcated in any of the public schools of the city but nothing in this section shall be construed to prohibit the reading of the Holy Scriptures.

Complainant: A patron of the schools, probably a Catholic sympathizer.

Cause for Complaint: Opening exercises in which the teacher repeated the Lord's Prayer and the Twenty-third Psalm. A pupil was expelled for refusing to refrain from regular work and preserve order during the exercises.

Issues Involved: 1. Were the exercises a form of religious worship? 2. Did the exercises constitute the teaching of sectarian or religious doctrine? 3. Do the constitution and the statute prohibit such exercises as a misuse of the public school funds?

Pertinent Factors: 1. There was no comment made upon the Scriptures. 2. Pupils were not required to participate in the exercises.

Holding of the Supreme Court: In announcing the unanimous decision of the Court the Justice said in part:

An examination of the evidence convinces us, as it convinced the learned judge who tried the cause, that the exercises of which plaintiff complained were not a form of religious worship, or the teaching of sectarian religious doctrine. There was not the slightest effort on the part of the teacher to inculcate any religious dogma. She repeated the Lord's Prayer and the Twenty-third Psalm, without response, comment, or remark. The pupils who desired gave their attention and took part, those who did not were at liberty to follow the wandering of their own imagination. There can be no question of the correctness of the legal premises of the plaintiff. Both our constitution and statutes prohibit all forms of religious worship or the teaching of sectarian or religious doctrine in the public schools. . . . However, there is nothing in the constitution or statute which can be construed as an intention to exclude the Bible from the public schools. . . . The noblest ideals of moral character are found in the Bible. To emulate these is the supreme conception of citizenship. It could not, therefore, have been the intention of the framers of our Constitution to impose the duty upon the legislature of establishing a system of common schools where morals were to be inculcated and exclude therefrom the lives of those persons who possessed the highest moral attainments.

KENTUCKY

State Constitutional Provisions Cited:

Sec. 5: No preference shall ever be given by law to any religious sect, society or denomination; nor to any particular creed, mode of worship or system of ecclesiastical polity; nor shall any person be compelled to attend any place of worship, to contribute to the erection or maintenance of any such place, or to the salary of any minister of religion; nor shall any man be compelled to send his child to any school to which he may be conscientiously opposed; and the civil rights, privileges or capacities of no person shall be taken away, or in any wise diminished or enlarged, on account of his belief or disbelief of any religious tenet, dogma or teaching. No human authority shall, in any case, whatever, control or interfere with the rights of conscience.

Sec. 189: No portion of any fund or tax now existing, or that may hereafter be raised or levied for educational purposes, shall be appropriated to, or used by, or in aid of any church, sectarian or denominational school.

Statutory Provisions Cited:

No books or other publications of a sectarian, infidel, or immoral character shall be used or distributed in any common school, nor shall any sectarian, infidel or immoral doctrine be taught therein. (Ky. Statutes 1903, Section 4368.)

Hackett v. *Brooksville School, 120 Ky. 608, (1905)*

Complainant: A patron who was probably a Catholic.

Cause for Complaint: The opening of a school by reading from King James Bible and reciting a particular general prayer.

Issues Involved: 1. Was the prayer sectarian? 2. Did the exercises make the school a "place of worship" or a "sectarian school"? 3. Was the teacher thereby made a "minister of religion"? 4. Is the King James Bible a sectarian book? 5. Did the exercises violate the constitution or the statute cited?

Pertinent Factors: 1. There was no comment on the Bible. 2. Pupils were not required to attend the exercises.

Holding of the Court of Appeals: By a unanimous decision the Court answered all the issues in the negative and denied an injunction against the exercises. The Court said in part:

As neither the form nor the substance of the prayer complained of seem to represent any peculiar view or dogma of any sect or denomination, or to teach them, or to detract from those of any other, it is not sectarian in the sense that the word is commonly used and understood, and as it was evidently intended in the section quoted. . . . Though it be conceded that any prayer is worship, and that public prayer is public worship, still appellant's children were not compelled to attend the place while the worshipping was done during the prayer. The school was not a "place of worship" nor are its teachers "ministers of religion" within the contemplation of section 5 of the Constitution, although a prayer may be offered incidentally at the opening of the school by a teacher. . . .

That the Bible, or any particular edition, has been adopted by one or more denominations as authentic, or by them asserted to be inspired, cannot make it a sectarian book. The book itself, to be sectarian, must show that it teaches the peculiar dogmas of a sect as such, and not alone that it is so comprehensive as to include them by the partial interpretation of its adherents. Nor is a book sectarian merely because it is edited or compiled by those of a particular sect. It is not the authorship nor mechanical composition of the book, nor the use of it, but its contents, that give it its character. . . .

We believe the reason and weight of the authorities support the view that the Bible is not of itself a sectarian book, and when used merely for reading in the common schools, without note or comment by teachers, is not sectarian instruction; nor does such use of the Bible make the schoolhouse a house of religious worship.

Williams v. *Board of Trustees, 173 Ky. 708, (1917)*

Complainants: Patrons who were probably Catholic sympathizers.

Cause of Complaint: 1. Designation of a Presbyterian school as the county high school. 2. Merging of a common school and a Presbyterian sectarian school.

Issues Involved: 1. Was there an appropriation of public funds in aid of a denominational and sectarian school? 2. Was the public school put under the influence, control and supervision of the sectarian school? 3. Did the arrangement violate the constitution and the statute?

Pertinent Factors: 1. This case was a rehearing of 172 Ky. 133. 2. The public school trustees merely paid the salaries of two teachers who were selected by the president of this sectarian school. This president controlled the entire school. The two teachers paid by the public simply taught grades six, seven and eight in the sectarian school building which was kept in repair by the public officials under the guise of rent or lease money for two rooms of the sectarian building. 3. Common-school pupils were not required to attend chapel exercises.

Holding of the Court of Appeals: The Court held that any arrangement whereby a sectarian school is designated as and accepted as a public school is prohibited by the constitution; that the constitution of Kentucky not only forbids such appropriation of public funds, as here shown, in aid of any sectarian school but it also contemplates that the separation between public schools and sectarian schools shall be open, notorious, and complete. The Court further said that even though public school pupils obtain advantages that they would not otherwise be able to have, and though a majority of the patrons approve of the arrangement, it is a violation of the constitution to bring, as in this case, a public school directly or indirectly, under the influence, control, or supervision of any sectarian institution or school. Injunction was ordered against the arrangement.

LOUISIANA

Herold v. *Parish Board, 136 La. 1034, (1915)*

State Constitutional Provisions Cited:

Art. 4: Every person has the natural right to worship God, according to the dictates of his conscience, and no law shall be passed respecting an establishment of religion.

Art. 53: No preference shall ever be given to, nor any discrimination made against any church, sect or creed of religion, or any form of religious faith or worship; . . .

Complainants: Two Jews and a Catholic, patrons of the public schools.

Cause for Complaint: 1. A school board resolution which provided for the reading of the Bible and the Lord's Prayer as opening exercises.

Issues Involved: 1. Do such exercises violate the right of liberty of conscience and freedom of worship? 2. Are such exercises sectarian worship? 3. Are such exercises a preference to Protestants and a discrimination against Catholics and Jews? 4. Are such exercises prohibited by the state constitution?

Pertinent Factors: 1. No particular version of the Bible designated. 2. No comment to be made on the reading. 3. Pupils to be excused upon request of parents.

Holding of the Supreme Court: By a unanimous decision the Court held that the exercises were violative of the right of conscience as to Jews but not as to Catholics and enjoined the enforcement of the resolution. The Court said in part:

And as the Court will not concern itself with the differences, or alleged errors, in the different translations of the Christian Bible, or the Bibles of the Christians, we cannot conclude that plaintiff Marston (Catholic) or his children would have their consciences violated by the reading of the Bible, or the offering of the Lord's Prayer. . . . And as he (the Jew) is guaranteed "the natural right to worship God, according to the dictates of his conscience," and as the resolution in question permits "lessons and truths" to be read or taught from the New Testament, particularly concerning the Son of God and His resurrection from the dead, etc., it gives a preference to the children of the Christian parents, and discriminates against the children of the Jews.

MAINE

Donahoe v. Richards, 38 Maine 379, (1854)

State Constitutional Provisions Cited:

Art. 1, Sec. 3: All men have a natural and inalienable right to worship Almighty God according to the dictates of their own consciences, and no one shall be hurt, molested, or restrained in his person, liberty, or estate for worshipping God in the manner and season most agreeable to the dictates of his own conscience, nor for his religious professions or sentiments, provided he does not disturb the public peace, nor obstruct others in their religious worship; and all persons demeaning themselves peaceably, as good members of the state, shall be equally under the protection of the laws, and no subordination or preference of any sect or denomination to another shall ever be established by law, nor shall any religious tests be required as a qualification for any office or trust under this state.

Complainant: A Catholic pupil of the public schools.

Cause for Complaint: Expulsion from school for refusal to obey the school officials and read from the King James Bible, the regularly adopted reading textbook.

Issues Involved: 1. Was the requirement to read from the King James Bible a violation of rights guaranteed by the constitution? 2. Was it an interference with the pupil's right of conscience? 3. Was the conscientious belief that such reading would be a sin a defense for refusing to comply with a constitutional requirement?

Pertinent Factors: 1. The King James Bible was purely a textbook, regularly adopted by the board acting according to the statute.

Holding of the Supreme Judicial Court: The unanimous decision of the Court was that the regulation adopting a particular version of the Bible as a textbook was constitutional and did not infringe upon the rights of conscience or the right to freedom of worship of the complainant. The pupil's conscientious belief was no excuse for disobedience. The Court closes its decision with this interesting declaration:

While the law should reign supreme, and obedience to its commands should ever be required, yet in the establishment of the law which is to control, there is no principle of wider application and of higher wisdom, commending itself alike to the broad field of legislative, and the more restricted one of municipal action . . . to those who enact the law, as well as those who, enjoying its benefits and privileges, should yield to its requirements, than a precept which is found with almost verbal identity in the versions (of the Bible) which, from education and association, are endeared to the respective parties in litigation:

"All things whatsoever ye would that men should do to you, do ye even so to them, for this is the law and the prophets."

MASSACHUSETTS

Spiller v. Inhabitants of Woburn, 94 Mass. 127, (1866)

State Constitutional Provisions Cited:

Part I, Art. 2: It is the right as well as the duty of all men in society, publicly, and at stated seasons to worship the Supreme Being, the great Creator and preserver of the Universe, and no Subject shall be hurt, molested, or restrained, in his Person, Liberty, or Estate, for worshipping God in the manner and season most agreeable to the Dictates of his own conscience, or for his religious Profession or sentiments; provided he doth not Disturb the public peace, or obstruct others in their religious worship.

Statutory Provisions Cited:

General Statutes, Chapter 38, No. 10, provided that one of the chief objects of education is

. . . to impress on the minds of children and youth committed to their care and instruction the principles of piety and justice, and a sacred regard for the truth.

Chapter 41, Number 9, provided that:

No one shall be excluded from a public school on account of his religious opinions.

Statute 1862, Chapter 57, requires that the daily reading of the Bible in public schools shall be without "written note or oral comment" and also that "no pupil shall be called upon to read any particular version, whose parent or guardian shall declare that he has conscientious scruples against allowing him to read therefrom."

Complainant: A pupil in a public school. Religious beliefs not given.

Cause for Complaint: Complainant was excluded from school for refusing to obey an order of the school committee that pupils should bow their heads during the daily reading of the Bible and prayer.

Issues Involved: 1. Did the school committee's order violate the constitution and the statutes? 2. Was the exclusion within their powers?

Pertinent Factor: The father had refused to request that his daughter be excused from bowing her head during the prayer.

Holding of the Supreme Judicial Court: The decision upheld the order of the board and the exclusion of the pupil as lawful. A part of the Court's opinion follows:

Having in view the manifest spirit and intention of these provisions (Constitutional and statutory), an order or a regulation by a school committee which would require a pupil to join in a religious rite or ceremony contrary to his or her religious opinions, or those of a parent or guardian, would be clearly unreasonable and invalid.

But we are unable to see that the regulation with which the plaintiff was required to comply can be justly said to fall within this category. In the first place, it did not prescribe an act which was necessarily one of devotion or religious ceremony. It went no further than to require the observance of quiet and decorum during the religious service with which the school was opened. It did not compel a pupil to join in the prayer, but only to assume an attitude which was calculated to prevent interruption by avoiding all communication with others during the service. In the next place the regulation did not require the pupil to comply with that part of it prescribing the position of the head during prayer, if the parent requested a child to be excused from it. This was an analogy to the provision already cited in relation to the reading of a particular version of the Bible, contained in St. 1862, c. 57, and takes away all ground of objection to the reasonableness and validity of the order.

MICHIGAN

Pfeiffer v. Board of Education of Detroit, 118 Mich. 560, (1898)

State Constitutional Provisions Cited:

Art. 4, Sec. 39, provides:

. . . The legislature shall pass no law to prevent any person from worshipping Almighty God according to the dictates of his own conscience, or to compel any person to attend, erect or support any place of religious worship, or to pay tithes, taxes, or other rates for the support of any minister of the gospel or teacher of religion.

Sec. 40 provides that

No money shall be appropriated or drawn from the treasury for the benefit of any religious sect or society, theological or religious seminary, nor shall property belonging to the state be appropriated for any such purpose.

Sec. 41 prohibits the legislature from

diminishing or enlarging the civil or political rights, privileges, and capacities of any person on account of his opinion or belief concerning matters of religion.

Complainant: No evidence as to his religious sympathies.

Cause of Complaint: The school board had adopted as a textbook "Readings from the Bible," from which teachers read to the pupils for fifteen minutes at the close of the school day.

Issues Involved: 1. Does the reading violate the constitution? 2. Does it constitute an "appropriation for the benefit of a religious or theological seminary"? 3. Are the "civil or political rights, privileges, and capacities" of any pupil "diminished or enlarged" thereby? 4. Has any pupil or any taxpayer been compelled to "attend, erect, or support any place of religious worship, or to pay tithes, taxes, or other rates for the support of any minister of the gospel or teacher of religion"? 5. Do the provisions of the Ordinance of 1787 have any weight in enjoining religious instruction upon the state?

Pertinent Factors: 1. A constitution must be construed with reference to the conditions prevailing at the time of its adoption. 2. The book used bore evidence that the compilers had attempted to group such Bible passages as should meet the approval of

Protestant, Catholic and Jew. 3. No comment. 4. Pupils might be excused from the readings.

Holding of the Supreme Court: In a divided decision the Court reversed the decision of the lower court which had granted the complainant a writ of mandamus, holding that none of the constitutional rights of complainant had been violated. A portion of the majority decision is as follows:

> I do not wish to be understood as assenting to the proposition that the ordinance of 1787 makes it imperative that religion shall be taught in the public schools. It was doubtless the opinion of the framers of that great document that public schools would of necessity tend to foster religion. But the extent to which I go is to say that the language of this instrument, when read in the light of the fact that this was at that date a Christian nation, is such as to preclude the idea that the framers of the constitution, "in conformity with the principles contained in the ordinance," intended, in the absence of a clear expression to that effect, to exclude wholly from the school all reference to the Bible.

The dissenting Judge said in part:

> As a result of it all, we find the language of our constitution, in its latest utterance, going further in the direction of separating religious instruction from the duty of the state than any language before used in any of the written constitutions. It was evidently the idea that the school system of the state should be so conducted that the children of Catholic and Protestant, Calvinist and Armenian, Hebrew and infidel, might attend its daily sessions, and obtain its benefits, without any discrimination being made in favor of one pupil against another, based upon the religious or want of belief of the parent. We all agree that children should be carefully educated in religion. They should be taught to fear God and love their fellow men. They should be made familiar with the truths of the Bible. They should be instructed to remember their Creator in the days of their youth, and to observe His commandments. But this is a branch of education which is not within the province of the state. It belongs to the parents, the home, the Sunday school, the mission, and the church.

Nebraska

State v. *Scheve, 65 Neb. 853, (1902)*

State Constitutional Provisions Cited:

Art. I, Sec. 4: All men have a natural and indefeasible right to worship Almighty God according to the dictates of their own conscience. No person shall be compelled to attend, erect, or support any place of worship, against his consent; and no preference shall be given, by law, to any religious society; nor shall any interference with the rights of conscience be permitted.

Art. VIII, Sec. 11: No sectarian instruction shall be allowed in any school or institution supported in whole or in part by the public funds set apart for educational purposes; nor shall the state accept any grant, conveyance, or bequest of money, lands, or other property to be used for sectarian purposes.

Complainant: A patron of the schools, probably a Catholic sympathizer.

Cause for Complaint: Reading of King James Bible, prayers and hymns.

Issues Involved: 1. Was sectarian religious instruction given? 2. Was there compulsory attendance on religious worship? 3. Was there an appropriation of public funds for sectarian instruction or purposes?

Pertinent Factors: 1. The teacher admitted that the services were religious services and conducted for that purpose.

Holding of the Supreme Court: The Court was unanimous in its decision that the exercises as conducted were forbidden by the constitution. One judge placed his decision entirely on the basis that the exercises as conducted were sectarian, while one judge was not agreed that the exercises constituted the schoolhouse a "place of worship." A part of the decision is:

Protestant sects who maintain, as a part of their ritual and discipline, stated weekly meetings, in which the exercises consist largely of prayers and songs and the reading or repetition of scriptural passages, would, no doubt, vehemently dissent from the proposition that such exercises are not devotional, or not in an exalted degree worshipful, or not intended for religious edification or instruction. That they possess all these features is a fact of such universal and familiar knowledge that the courts will take judicial notice of it without formal proof. That such exercises are also sectarian in their character is not less free from doubt.

Upon overruling a motion for a rehearing in 1903, the Court made a statement of its position, seeming to weaken its former position somewhat. A part of this statement follows:

7. The law does not forbid the use of the Bible in the public schools; it is not proscribed either by the constitution or the statutes;

and the courts have no right to declare its use to be unlawful because
it is possible or probable that those who are privileged to use it will
misuse the privilege by atempting to propagate their own peculiar
theological or ecclesiastical views or dogmas.

8. The point where the courts may rightfully interfere to prevent
the use of the Bible in a public school is where legitimate use has
degenerated into abuse—where a teacher employed to give secular instruction has violated the constitution by becoming a sectarian propa-
gandist.

9. Whether it is prudent or politic to permit Bible reading in the
public schools is a question for the school authorities, but whether
the practice of Bible reading has taken the form of sectarian instruction
is a question for the courts to determine upon evidence.

New York

The records of the office of the chief executive officer of the
schools of New York reveal many traces of the controversy over
religious influence in the public schools.   Since the State Superintendent was given authority to decide all controversies regarding the administration of the common schools by legislative
action in 1822, successive superintendents have had to pass upon
many cases involving religious and sectarian influence.   The most
important decisions made between 1822 and 1913 are to be found
in the Annual Report of the University of the State of New
York, Volume 2, entitled *Judicial Decisions,* prepared by Thomas
E. Finegan, Ph.D., and published in 1914.   On page 532 it is
shown that Superintendent Dix in 1837 held that a teacher might
open his school with prayer, provided that the pupils were not
compelled to be present at the time and the prayer did not con-
sume time regularly allotted to instruction.   On page 526 a
decision of the same purport, made by Superintendent Spencer in
1839, is given.   This same policy is adhered to by Superintendent
Rice in a decision rendered in 1866 and reported on page 527.
Superintendent Gilmour reiterated this same policy in a decision
made in 1870 and reported on page 525.   In a decision by Superintendent Weaver in 1870 and reported on page 524 it was held
that school trustees had no legal right to direct that the King
James Bible be read to pupils during school hours or to expel
pupils for refusing to attend such reading.   This same position
was again taken by Superintendent Weaver in Case 1985, decided in 1872 and reported on page 528.   In this decision Super-

intendent Weaver adhered to the principle of the earlier decisions. He maintained, nevertheless, that, while there was no
rightful authority in the law to permit the use of any portion of
the regular school hours for religious exercises and to compel the
pupils to attend, however, there was nothing to prevent the
reading of the Bible or the holding of other religious exercises
in the presence of such pupils as might voluntarily attend at
other than regular school hours. Superintendent Ruggles in a
decision reported on page 531 and made in 1884 adhered to the
policy of his predecessors. Commissioner Draper continued this
same policy in a decision given in 1909 and reported on page 527.

A different phase of this controversy regarding religious and
sectarian influence in the public schools is brought out by the
decisions of the Superintendents on the matter of the wearing
of distinctive religious garb by Catholic sisters when teaching
in the public schools and the question of maintaining public
schools in buildings owned by religious organizations. In Case
3520, reported on page 533 of the annual report before referred
to, Superintendent Draper in 1887 said in part:

But the school which the board maintains in this property must be,
in all regards, a *public* school. . . . I have given the question raised
in relation to the dress of the teachers and the names (Sister Mary,
etc.,) by which they are known among the pupils very full consideration, and have arrived at the conclusion that the wearing of an unusual
garb, worn exclusively by members of one religious sect, and for the
purpose of indicating membership in that sect, by the teachers in
a public school, constitutes a sectarian influence which ought not to be
persisted in.

In 1896 Superintendent Skinner decided (Case 4516, page 538
of the report previously referred to) that the policy of the school
law demanded that each school district of the State should become the owner of a schoolhouse and that rooms should be leased
for the purpose of maintaining schools only in emergencies; that
it was the duty of school officials to require that no teacher
should wear the distinctive dress of any religious sect or order
while in the public school rooms and performing her duties as
a teacher.

Superintendent Skinner upheld this policy in the following
cases: *Case 4546, Kennedy* v. *Board of Education,* (1897) page
554; *Keyser* v. *Board of Education,* Case 4722 (1898), page 560;

Case 4642, Lockwood v. *Board of Education (1898)*, page 568; *Bates* v. *Sylvester,* Case 5010, (1902) page 572.

O'Connor v. *Hendrick, 184 N. Y. 421 (1906)*

State Constitutional Provisions Cited:

Art. IX, Sec. 4. N. Y. Const.: Neither the state nor any subdivision thereof shall use its property or credit or any public money, or authorize or permit either to be used, directly or indirectly, in aid or maintenance, other than for examination or inspection, of any school or institution of learning wholly or in part under the control or direction of any religious denomination, or in which any denominational tenet or doctrine is taught.

Concerning Statutory Provisions:

While it is true that there is no express grant of authority to the state superintendent of public instruction in the Consolidated School Law (Laws N. Y. 1894, Ch. 556, Sec. I) to establish regulations as to the management of the common schools, the existence of a general power of supervision on his part over such schools is clearly implied in many parts of the statute. (Body of the Decision.)

Complainant: O'Connor, a Catholic sister and a teacher in the public schools. One Bates prosecuted an appeal under the statute to review the action of Hendrick as school trustee in allowing the sister to continue to teach while wearing her garb.

Cause for Complaint: The withholding of the salary of the sister because of disobeying the State Superintendent's order against the wearing of distinctive religious garb in the schoolroom.

Issues Involved: 1. Is the influence of the garb of a Catholic sister, when teaching in the public school room, sectarian? 2. Does the wearing of such a garb in the public school room amount to sectarian teaching? 3. Does the wearing of such religious garb violate the provisions of Article IX, Sec. 4 of the state constitution, forbidding the use of the property or credit of the state in aid of sectarian influences?

Pertinent Factors: 1. The Appellate Division of the Supreme Court, 96 N. Y. S. 161 (1905), had decided in its hearing of this case that the saying of Catholic prayers by a sister in her garb, during the school session, although the non-Catholic pupils were not required to be present, constituted religious teaching.

2. During the succeeding year the defendant, Hendrick, allowed the sister to continue teaching, contrary to the order of the State Superintendent.

Holding of the New York Court of Appeals: [1] 1. Judgment of the lower court affirmed. 2. The order of the Superintendent was a reasonable and valid exercise of the power conferred upon him.

The Court said in part:

Here (Const. Art. IX, Sec. 4) we have the plainest possible declaration of the public policy of the state as opposed to the prevalence of sectarian influences in the public schools. The regulation established by the state superintendent of public instruction through the agency of his order in the Bates appeal is in accord with the public policy thus evidenced by the fundamental law. There can be little doubt that the effect of the costume worn by these Sisters of St. Joseph at all times in the presence of their pupils would be to inspire respect if not sympathy for the religious denomination to which they manifestly belong. To this extent the influence was sectarian, even if it did not amount to the teaching of denominational doctrine.

The Matter of Roche, 26 N. Y. St. Dept. Rep. 217 (1921)

Constitutional Provisions Cited:

The free exercise and enjoyment of religious profession and worship, without discrimination or preference, shall forever be allowed in this State to all mankind; . . . (Art. I, Sec. 3, N. Y. Const.)

Complainant: Roche, a Catholic priest.

Cause for Complaint: The holding of public school in the Sunday school room of the Christian church.

Issues Involved: 1. Does the compulsory attendance of Catholic pupils in this room amount to an interference with their freedom of worship?

Pertinent Factors: 1. This was an emergency use caused by the burning of the high school building. 2. No visible evidences of sectarian influence.

Holding of the Court: In denying the complainant's contention:

The doctrine of freedom of worship as declared in the State Constitution should not be applied so as to prevent, in case of emergency,

[1] The New York Court of Appeals is the highest court in the New York Judiciary System. New York has several courts of the Appellate Division of the Supreme Court that are sometimes mistaken for the highest court.

the use of a suitable room in a building owned by a religious corporation for school purposes. The use of such a room for school purposes, under the conditions shown to exist in this case, does not constitute the imparting of religious instruction or influence in the public schools and may not be prevented on the grounds of its illegality.

Stein v. *Brown, 211 N. Y. S. 822, (1925)*

State Constitutional Provisions Cited: Art. IX, Sec. 4 (quoted above).

Statutory Provisions Cited: Sec. 621 of the Education Law (as amended by Laws 1921, c. 386, sec. 2, and known as the Compulsory Education Law) provides:

1. Every child within the compulsory school ages . . . in proper physical and mental condition to attend school, who resides in a city or school district having a population of 4500 or more and employing a superintendent of schools, shall regularly attend upon instruction for the entire time during which the schools of such city or district are in session as follows; . . .

Complainant: A taxpayer. No statement as to religious belief.

Cause of Complaint: Dismissal by the school authorities of pupils, upon request of parents, to attend regular religious instruction at local churches.

Issues Involved: 1. May the rulings of the Board of Education be attacked only before the Commissioner of Education and is his decision in such appeals, petitions or proceedings final and conclusive, and not subject to question or review in any place or court whatever? 2. Did the use of the local school's printing presses upon which to print the cards which parents used to notify teachers as to what church the parents desired their children to attend and which the church teachers used to notify the public school teachers as to who had attended religious instruction, constitute a violation of Art. IX, Sec. 4 of the constitution? 3. Was it a violation of the Compulsory Attendance Law for school authorities to excuse pupils for 45 minutes each week to receive religious instruction for a definite and fixed period weekly?

Pertinent Factors: 1. In this particular case there seems to be no question of any one denomination exercising control over the schools. The statement of the issues gives the pertinent facts involved.

Holding of the Appellate Division of the Supreme Court: 1. In reference to the first issue the Court said in part:

This does not apply to a cause of action on the part of a taxpayer for an improper use of the funds and property of the board of education or for the determination of constitutional questions or illegal acts on the part of officials. Such questions are always for the courts.

With reference to the factor of sectarian influence and issue number 2, the Court said in part:

The fact that no particular denomination was favored or intended so to be by this action of the board of education does not affect the question. The fact is that the property of the board was permitted to be used directly in aid of such schools of religious instruction whose members saw fit to avail themselves of the action taken by the defendants. It seems perfectly clear that it was illegal for the defendants to permit the printing of the cards to be done on its presses.

With reference to the third issue the Court said in part:

I find nothing whatsoever in the Education Law authorizing either the board of education, the State Commissioner of Education, or the Education Department to change, limit, or shorten the time of attendance of pupils in public schools, except the provisions of Chapter 689, Laws of 1917, authorizing the Commissioner of Education to suspend for the period between the 1st day of April and the 1st day of November of each year "for the purpose of aiding and performing labor in the cultivation, production and care of food products upon farms and gardens within the state . . . subject to such condition," etc. "as may be imposed by the Commissioner of Education, and shall be subject to rules and regulations prescribed by him."

In general the Court said in part:

Education Law, sec. 620 . . . prescribes the instruction required in public schools. Religious education is not one of them. Consequently it would be unlawful and unauthorized for a board of education to substitute religious instruction in the school in the place of the instruction required. . . .

The courts of this state and other states, whenever the question has arisen, have uniformly discountenanced attempts to join religious instruction with the instruction prescribed for the public schools.

. . . In many school districts in the state there is only one church sufficiently near to the school to be reached by the children attending that school. Similar action taken in such localities would favor that church, whatever its denomination. Should it happen that all or nearly all the children or their parents be members of such congregation and avail themselves of the action of the board of education, the action would simply result in shortening the school hours. . . .

There is another objection to the plan. Pupils who leave the school weekly for religious instruction are likely to fall behind those that remain the full time, . . .

Lewis v. Graves, Unofficial Report from the Press

According to unofficial reports in the press, on April 24, 1926, Justice Staley of one of the courts of the Appellate Division of the New York Supreme Court rendered a decision in a case similar to that of *Stein* v. *Brown,* with the exception that no cards had been printed by the school for use in excusing the pupils. Justice Staley, in upholding this practice of thus excusing pupils for attendance upon religious instruction, is unofficially reported as saying in part:

The facts in this case establish no violation of this constitutional prohibition. The mere excusing of pupils at the volition of their parents for a half hour period each week to attend religious instruction outside the school and at places unrelated to school activities, in the free exercise and enjoyment of their religious profession, does not constitute the use of public property, credit or money in aid of any institution of learning under the control of any religious denomination.

The thing prohibited by the constitution is the use of public property and money for the designated purpose, and where there is no such use, there is no basis for just claim of constitutional violation.

In that respect this proceeding differs materially from the facts in the Mount Vernon Case (*Stein* v. *Brown*) where public property was used for the printing of the excuse cards, which were printed by the School of Industrial Arts by the pupils therein, and that action was declared "unlawful and in violation of the State Constitution."

The requirement of the compulsory attendance law for attendance during the entire time during which public schools are in session is not an arbitrary provision, but is qualified by the allowance of occasional absences not amounting to irregular attendance in the fair meaning of the term.

These absences are permitted by law upon excuses allowed by the general rules and practice of such school. These rules are prescribed by the Board of Education in the performance of their duties.

It may interest the reader to know that the newspaper report of this case credits its prosecution, as well as that of *Stein* v. *Brown*, to the Free Thinkers Society of New York City, a society that may be classed as being composed of non-believers in the Bible.

NORTH DAKOTA

Pronovost v. *Brunette, 36 N. D. 288, (1917)*

State Constitutional Provisions Cited:

The free exercise and enjoyment of religious profession and worship, without discrimination or preference, shall be forever guaranteed in this state, and no person shall be rendered incompetent to be a witness or juror on account of his opinion on matters of religious belief; but the liberty of conscience hereby secured shall not be so construed as to excuse acts of licentiousness, or justify practices inconsistent with the peace or safety of this state.

Statutory Provisions Cited: The statutes provided that whenever there were nine children residing two and one-half miles from a public school house, additional school accommodations might be provided by the officials.

Complainants: Two Catholic school directors who with the defendant composed the local board.

Cause for Complaint: Defendant, the third school director, refused to give up the keys to the school building which the district had voted, 33 to 2, to abandon and to move the public school to a room owned by a Catholic Convent.

Issues Involved: 1. Would such action result in restraint of freedom of worship of non-Catholic pupils? 2. Would the action result in sectarian influence and instruction?

Pertinent Factors: 1. Here was an attempt to abandon an adequate building and lease a room in a sectarian building which was connected with the Catholic church. 2. There were not nine pupils living more than two and one-half miles from a public school.

Holding of the Supreme Court: Judgment for the defendant. The Court held it to be the legislative policy in the state that the public schools in the common-school districts should be maintained in buildings owned by the public.

Ohio

Board of Education of Cincinnati v. Minor, 23 Ohio St. 211,
(1872)

State Constitutional Provisions Cited:

Art. I, Sec. 7: All men have a natural and indefeasible right to worship Almighty God according to the dictates of their own conscience. No person shall be compelled to attend, erect, or support any place of worship, against his consent; and no preference shall be given, by law, to any religious society; nor shall any interference with the rights of conscience be permitted. . . . Religion, morality, and knowledge, however, being essential to good government, it shall be the duty of the general assembly to pass suitable laws to protect every religious denomination in the peaceable enjoyment of its mode of public worship, and to encourage schools and the means of instruction.

Art. II, Sec. 6: The general assembly shall make such provisions, by taxation or otherwise, as, with the income arising from the school trust fund, will secure a thorough and efficient system of common schools throughout the state; but no religious or other sect or sects shall ever have any exclusive right to, or control of, any part of the school funds of this state.

Complainants: Taxpayers. No indication of their religious beliefs.

Cause of Complaint: The board of education passed a resolution which provided that a former resolution, which permitted the reading of the Bible in the public schools, should be repealed and the practice abolished.

Issues Involved as Stated by the Court:

The case, as we view it, presents merely or mainly a question of the court's rightful authority to interfere in the management and control of the public schools of the state. In other words, the real question is, has the court jurisdiction to interfere in the management and control of such schools, to the extent of enforcing religious instructions, or the reading of religious books therein.

Pertinent Factors: 1. Under the old rule of the board, children might read from any version of the Scriptures that their parents desired them to use. 2. There was no note or comment on the reading. 3. There were no pertinent statutory provisions on the matter. 4. The content of no regular textbook was affected.

Holding of the Supreme Court: By a unanimous decision the Court's right to interfere in the management or control of the schools was denied and the board's right to pass and enforce such resolutions was sustained.

The attitude of the Court is shown by the following:

To enjoin "instructions" in knowledge, the knowledge of truth in all its branches . . . religious, moral and otherwise, . . . is one thing; and to declare what is truth—truth in any one, or in all departments of human knowledge,—and to enjoin the teaching of that, as truth, is quite another thing. To enjoin the latter, would be to declare that human knowledge had reached its ultimatum. This the constitution does not undertake to do, neither as to "religion," "morality," nor any other branch or department of human knowledge. . . .

The truth is that these are matters left to legislative discretion, subject to the limitations on legislative power, regarding religious freedom, contained in the bill of rights; and subject also to the injunction that laws shall be passed, such as in the judgment of the legislature are "suitable" to encourage general means of instruction, including, among other means, a system of common schools.

Equally plain it is to us, that if the supposed injunction to provide for religious instructions is to be found in the clauses of the constitution in question, it is one that rests exclusively upon the legislature.

The real claim here is, that by "religion" in this clause (sec. 7) of the constitution, is meant "Christian religion," and that by "religious denomination" in the same clause is meant "Christian denomination." If this claim is well founded, I do not see how we can consistently avoid giving a like meaning to the same words and their cognates, "worship," "religious society," "sect," conscience," "religious belief," throughout the entire section. To do so, it will readily be seen, would be to withdraw from every person not of Christian belief the guaranties therein vouch-safed, and to withdraw many of them from Christians themselves. . . .

Nessle v. Hun, Ohio Nisi Prius 140, (1894)

That the position taken by the Supreme Court in *Board of Education* v. *Minor* was accepted as the law in Ohio as late as 1894 is shown by the decision of the above county court case. In this case a local school board passed a resolution providing that the Bible should be read in its schools. The Court held that, under section 3985 of the statute, which provided "that the board of each district shall make rules and regulations as it may deem expedient and necessary for its government and the government of its appointees and the pupils," the courts have no power to interfere against the resolution providing that the Bible be read.   This Court also held that the question of the teaching of the Bible was not even raised under the pleadings.

PENNSYLVANIA

Hysong v. School District, 164 Pa. St. 629, (1894)

State Constitutional Provisions Cited:

Art. I, Sec. 3: All men have a natural and indefeasible right to worship Almighty God according to the dictates of their own consciences; no man can of right be compelled to attend, erect or support any place of worship, or to maintain any ministery, against his consent; no human authority can, in any case whatever, control or interfere with the rights of conscience and no preference shall ever be given by law to any religious establishments or modes of worship.

Sec. 4: No person who acknowledges the being of a God, and a future state of rewards and punishments shall, on account of his religious sentiments, be disqualified to hold any office or place of trust or profit under this Commonwealth.

Complainants: Patrons of the schools, probably Protestants.

Causes of Complaint: 1. Alleged sectarian teaching in public schools.   2. The employment of teachers, sisters of a Catholic society, who taught in their religious garb.

Issues Involved: 1. Would the exclusion of a Sister of Charity from employment as a teacher in the public schools, because she is a Roman Catholic, be a violation of the spirit of the Constitution as cited?   2. Does the wearing of the religious garb of a Catholic sister constitute sectarian teaching?

Pertinent Factors: 1. There was no sectarian instruction during the regular school hours but there was such instruction after hours.   2. The lower court had forbidden any sectarian instruction in the school building.

Holding of the Supreme Court: By a divided decision the Court held that the first issue should be answered in the affirmative and the second in the negative and affirmed the decision of the lower Court.   A part of the majority opinion follows:

Inevitably, in a popular government by the majority, public institutions will be tinged, more or less, by the religious proclivities of the majority; but in all cases where a discretion is reposed by law, we must assume in the absence of evidence to the contrary, that the public officer performed his duty.

. . . that it is sectarian teaching for a devout woman to appear in a school room in a dress peculiar to a religious organization of a Christian church. We decline to do so; the law does not so say. The legislature may, by statute, enact that all teachers shall wear in the school room a particular style of dress, and that none other shall be worn, and thereby secure the same uniformity of outward appearance as we now see in city police, railroad trainmen, and nurses of some of our large hospitals.

From the dissenting opinion:

They (Sisters) wear, and they must wear, at all times, a prescribed, unchangeable, ecclesiastical dress which was plainly intended to proclaim their non-secular and religious character, their particular church and order, and their separation from the world. They come into the schools, not as common-school teachers, or as civilians, but as the representatives of a particular order in a particular church whose lives have been dedicated to religious work under the direction of that church. Now the point of the objection is not that their religion disqualifies them. It does not. It is not that holding an ecclesiastical office or position disqualifies them, for it does not. It is the introduction into the schools as teachers of persons who are by their striking and distinctive ecclesiastical robes necessarily and constantly asserting their membership in a particular church and in a religious order within that church, and the subjection of their lives to the direction and control of its officers. . . . If a school so conducted is not dominated by sectarian influence, and under sectarian control, it is not easy to see how it could be.

Commonwealth v. *Herr, 229 Pa. St. 132, (1910)*

Sixteen years after the decision in *Hysong* v. *School District* the Pennsylvania Court was called upon to decide the constitutionality of a statute entitled:

An Act to prevent the wearing in the public schools of this Commonwealth, by any of the teachers thereof, of any dress, insignia, marks or emblems indicating the fact that such teacher is an adherent or member of any religious order, sect or denomination, and imposing a fine upon the board of directors of any school permitting the same.

Defendant Herr was indicted for the violation of this law. He had permitted Sisters of the Catholic church to teach while wearing their distinctive religious garb. In holding the statute constitutional by a unanimous decision the Court said in part:

The right of the individual to clothe himself in whatever garb his taste, his inclination, the tenets of his sect, or even his religious sentiments may dictate is no more absolute than his right to give utterance to his sentiments, religious or otherwise. In neither case can it be said that a statute cannot restrain him from exercising these rights whenever, wherever and in whatever manner he conscientiously believes it to be his moral or religious duty to do so.

TEXAS

Church v. Bullock, 109 S. W. (Texas) 115, (1908)

State Constitutional Provisions Cited:

Art. I, Sec. 6: All men have a natural and indefeasible right to worship Almighty God according to the dictates of their own consciences. No man shall be compelled to attend, erect or support any place of worship, or to maintain any ministery against his consent. No human authority ought, in any case whatever, to control or interfere with the rights of conscience in matters of religion, and no preference shall ever be given by law to any religious society or mode of worship. But it shall be the duty of the legislature to pass such laws as may be necessary to protect equally every religious denomination in the peaceable enjoyment of its own mode of public worship.

Sec. 7: No money shall be appropriated or drawn from the treasury for the benefit of any sect, or religious society, theological or religious seminary; nor shall property belonging to the state be appropriated for any such purposes.

Art. VIII, Sec. 5: . . . nor shall the same, or any part thereof, ever be appropriated to or used for the support of any sectarian school. . . .

Complainants: Patrons of the public schools, one an unbeliever in the Bible, two Jews, and two Catholics.

Cause of Complaint: 1. The reading of the King James Bible, the reciting of the Lord's Prayer, and the singing of songs, mostly patriotic.

Issues Involved: 1. Did the exercises constitute the schools a "sect," "religious society," "theological seminary," "place of worship," or the teachers "ministers of religion," or make the public schools "sectarian" within the meaning of the articles of the Constitution quoted?

Pertinent Factors: 1. There was no comment on the exercises. 2. All pupils were required to be present and to be orderly. 3. They were asked but not required to participate. 4. They were requested but not compelled to stand and bow their heads during the time the prayer was being recited.

Holding of the Supreme Court: By a unanimous decision, the exercises were held not to be a violation of any of the constitutional provisions.

Parts of the decision follow:

To hold that the offering of prayers, either by the repetition of the Lord's Prayer, or otherwise, the singing of songs, whether devotional or not, and the reading of the Bible, make the place where such is done a place of worship, would produce intolerable results . . . in fact, Christianity is so interwoven with the web and woof of the state government that to sustain the contention that the Constitution prohibits reading the Bible, offering prayers, or singing songs of a religious character in any public building of the government would produce a condition bordering upon moral anarchy. The absurd and hurtful consequences furnish a strong argument against the soundness of the proposition.

The right to instruct the young in the morality of the Bible might be carried to such an extent in the public schools as would make it obnoxious to the constitutional inhibition, but not because God is worshipped, but because by the character of the services the place would be made a "place of worship."

. . . One or more individuals do not have the right to have the courts deny the people the privilege of having their children instructed in the public schools in the moral truths of the Bible, because such objectors do not desire that their own children shall be participants therein.

VERMONT

Ferriter v. *Tyler, 48 Vermont 444, (1876)*

State Constitutional Provisions Cited:

Art. III: That all men have a natural and inalienable right to worship Almighty God according to the dictates of their own consciences and understandings, as in their opinion shall be regulated by the word of God; and that no man ought to, or of right can, be compelled to attend any religious worship, etc., contrary to the dictates of his conscience; nor can any man be justly deprived or abridged of any civil right as a citizen on account of his religious sentiments or peculiar mode of religious worship; and no authority can or ought to be vested in or assumed by any power whatever that shall in any case interfere with, or in any manner control, the rights of conscience in the free exercise of religious worship; nevertheless, every sect or denomination of Christians ought to observe the Sabbath or Lord's day, and keep up some sort of religious worship, which to them shall seem most agreeable to the revealed will of God.

Statutory Provisions Cited: The statutes charge the school committee with the duty of

. . . adopting all requisite measures for the inspection, examination, and regulation of the schools and to the improvement of scholars in learning.

Complainants: Patrons who were Catholics.

Cause of Complaint: The exclusion of pupils from school for absence, contrary to the rule of the school committee, while attending Catholic religious services on Corpus Christi day.

Issues Involved: 1. Did the enforcement of the rule of exclusion violate the rights of pupils under Art. III of the Constitution?   2. Is the right of the committee to enforce attendance superior to that of the parent to control the moral training and culture of the child?

Pertinent Factors: 1. The absence was at the direction of the priest.   2. The pupils had notice that their absence would not be excused.   3. The school officials demanded assurance that such absences would not be repeated as the condition upon which pupils might return to school.

Holding of the Supreme Court: The rule of the committee was sustained on both questions.   The Court said in part:

Let it be repeated, then, that that article in the Constitution was not designed to exempt any person or persons of any sect, on the score of conscience as to matters of religion, from the operation and obligatory force of the general laws of the state, authorized by other portions of the same instrument, and designed to serve the purposes contemplated by such other portions; it was not designed to exempt any persons from the same subjection that others are under to the laws and their administration, on the score that such subjection at times would interfere with the performance of religious rites, and the observance of religious ordinances, which they would deem it their duty to perform and observe but for such subjection. . . .

WASHINGTON

State v. *Frazier, 102 Wash. 369, (1918)*

State Constitutional Provisions Cited:

Art. I, Sec. 11: No public money or property shall be appropriated for, or applied to, any religious worship, exercise or instruction, or the support of any religious establishment.

Amendment to Art. I, Sec. 11: Provided, however, that this article shall not be so construed as to forbid the employment by the state of a chaplain for the state penitentiary and for such of the state reformatories as in the discretion of the legislature may seem justified.

Art. IX, Sec. 4: All schools maintained or supported wholly or in part by the public funds shall be forever free from sectarian control or influence.

Complainant: A high school pupil.

Cause for Complaint: Frazier, superintendent of city schools, refused to give an examination in a course in outside Bible study and also to give those who should pass the examination high school credit toward graduation.

Issues Involved: 1. Would the action sought to be enforced by mandamus constitute an expenditure of public funds for "any religious worship, exercise, or instruction, or the support of any religious establishment" within the prohibition of the Constitution?

Pertinent Factors: 1. The State Board of Education had passed a resolution commending the allowing of credits in high school for Bible study done outside of school. 2. It had appointed a committee to consider a plan for allowing such credit and issuing a syllabus of Bible study under the auspices of the State Board of Education, together with rules and regulations for distributing examination questions at least once each year. 3. This plan was already in effect in several large cities in the state. 4. The only thing that the school was to do was to furnish the syllabus, give the examination, rate the papers, and determine the credit.

Holding of the Supreme Court: The complainant's petition for mandamus was denied by a unanimous decision. The issue was decided in the affirmative. A part of the decision follows:

The framers of the Constitution were not content to declare that our public schools should be kept free from sectarian control or influence;

they went further and made it certain that their declaration should not be overcome by changing sentiments or opinions. They declared that "no public money or property shall ever be appropriated or applied to any religious worship, exercise or instruction," and in this respect our Constitution differs from any other that has been called to our attention.

Concerning the cases from other states, cited by counsel, the Court remarked:

But these cases are cited upon provisions that go no further than Art. IX, Sec. 4, of our Constitution. Their purpose is to prevent the appropriation of money for parochial and denominational schools; a privilege that has been abused by the legislatures of some of the states, and of which the people were no doubt mindful at the time our constitution was adopted. In the light of other constitutions, the abuses in other states, and the evident purpose of the framers of the Constitution to save some of the questions which had there arisen, there can be no doubt that more was intended than a simple declaration that our schools should be kept free from sectarian influences.

The Court also pointed to the amendment to Art. I, Sec. 11, as conclusive evidence of the understanding of the provisions of the constitution.

WISCONSIN

State Constitutional Provisions Cited:

Art. I, Sec. 18: The right of every man to worship Almighty God according to the dictates of his own conscience shall never be infringed; nor shall any man be compelled to attend, erect, or support any place of worship, or to maintain any minister against his consent; nor shall any control of or interference with the rights of conscience be permitted, or any preference be given, by law, to any religious establishments or modes of worship; nor shall any money be drawn from the treasury for the benefit of religious societies, or religious or theological seminaries.

Art. X, Sec. 3: The legislature shall provide by law for the establishment of district schools, which shall be as nearly uniform as practicable, and such schools shall be free, and without charge for tuition to all children between the ages of four and twenty years; and no sectarian instruction shall be allowed therein.

Weiss v. *District Board, 76 Wis. 177, (1890)*

Complainant: Patrons of the schools who were Catholics.

Cause for Complaint: The reading of the King James Bible as a textbook.

Issues Involved: 1. Did the reading of the entire Bible constitute sectarian instruction within the meaning of the Constitution Art. X, Sec. 3?   2. Did it violate Sec. 3, Ch. 251, Laws
of 1883, which provides that "no textbooks shall be permitted
in any free public schools which will have a tendency to inculcate
sectarian ideas"?   3. Did the reading violate the "rights of conscience" of pupils or result in "withdrawing money from the state
treasury for the benefit of a religious school," within the meaning of Art. I, Sec. 18?

Pertinent Factors: 1. The Bible as a whole had been regularly adopted as a textbook.   2. Children were not required to
attend the reading.   3. There was no comment on the reading.
4. The petitioners claimed that the Catholic Church has divine
authority as the only infallible teacher and interpreter of the
Bible.

Holding of the Supreme Court: By a unanimous decision all
the issues were answered in the affirmative and the petition for
mandamus against the reading was sustained.   A part of the
opinion follows:

The term sectarian instruction in the constitution manifestly refers
exclusively to instruction in religious doctrines, and the prohibition is
only aimed at such instruction as is sectarian; that is to say, instruction
in religious doctrines which are believed by some religious sects and
rejected by others.   Hence, to teach the existence of a supreme being
of infinite wisdom, power, and goodness, and that it is the highest duty
of all men to adore, obey, and love him, is not sectarian, because all
religious sects so believe and teach.   The instruction becomes sectarian
when it goes further and inculcates doctrines or dogma concerning
which the religious sects are in conflict.   This we understand to be the
meaning of the constitutional prohibition.

There is much in the Bible which cannot be characterized as sectarian.
There can be no valid objection to the use of such matter in the
secular instruction of pupils.   Much of it has great historical or literary
value which may be thus utilized without violating the constitutional
prohibition.   It may also be used to inculcate good morals—that is, our
duties to each other—which may and ought to be inculcated by the
district schools.

So long as our constitution remains as it is, no one's religion can be
taught in our common schools.   By religion I mean religion as a system,
not religion in the sense of natural law.   Religion in the latter sense
is the source of all law and government, justice and truth.   Religion

as a system of belief cannot be taught without offense to those who have their own peculiar views of religion, no more than it can be without offense to the different sects of religion. . ... .

It is said if reading the Protestant Bible in school is offensive to parents of some of the scholars, and antagonistic to their own religious views, their children can retire. They ought not to be compelled to go out of school for such a reason for one moment. The suggestion itself concedes the whole argument.

Dorner v. *School District, 137 Wis. 147, (1908)*

This case arose out of a situation which might have presented definite questions concerning sectarian instruction and influence had they been presented by the appeal to the Supreme Court. A district school had been carried on for twenty years in a parochial school building. All but one or two pupils were Catholics. Dorner, who had lived in the district for years, finally brought a suit to enjoin the continuance of the arrangement and to recover money paid to the Catholic organization. The school directors had understood the arrangement but as no one had ever before objected they had considered the arrangement satisfactory.

The Court granted the injunction against the continuance of this arrangement but refused to rule that the holding of a public school in a church building was necessarily illegal. It also refused to allow the recovery from the church on the ground that a court of equity may and should refuse to upset consummated and contemplated transactions to the hurt of those who have acted in good faith, at the suit of one who, by laches or failure to protest such action before its consummation, has induced or justified a belief that he acquiesced in and approved the action of which he now complains.

State v. *District Board, 162 Wis. 482, (1916)*

State Constitutional Provisions Cited: Art. I, Sec. 18; Art. X, Sec. 3. (See page 109.)

Complainant: Patrons of the school, probably Catholics.

Cause for Complaint: 1. The practice of holding commencements of the public schools in churches and inviting ministers or priests to offer an invocation or prayer at these exercises.

Issues Involved: 1. Did the exercises violate the constitutional provisions which prohibit (a) sectarian instruction in the public schools, (b) compulsion in the support of "any minister" or "attendance upon any place of worship."

Pertinent Factors: 1. Ministers or priests were not paid for their services. 2. No rental was paid for the church. 3. No complaint had ever been made that any minister or priest had ever shown any hint or suggestions of sectarianism in his prayer. 4. Graduates were not compelled to attend the exercises.

Holding of the Supreme Court: The Court held that none of the rights guaranteed by the Constitution had been violated. The Judge gave considerable space to the ethical features of the case as distinguished from the legal rights. He advised the avoidance of such difficulties through the observance of discretion on the part of officials in avoiding and discontinuing such practices when any substantial number of patrons objected to them. He observed:

It is not wise or politic to do certain things, at all times, although no legal rights would be invaded by doing them. . . .

Considering what has been done here and the rare occasions on which it has been done or can be done, the matter complained of seems to be inconsequential to furnish the subject of a lawsuit.

THE TREND OF THE DECISIONS

Undoubtedly the general trend of the decisions over the United States has been from a point at which only sectarian or denominational instruction was construed as unconstitutional and illegal in the public schools toward a point at which the entire elimination of any religious instruction as such, or religious influence whatsoever, is intended.

New York is the only state in which there have been enough judicial decisions on these issues to indicate any trend within the state itself. In that state the head of the State Department of Education, whose decisions are final and not subject to review by any court, has had such cases before him frequently. The trend of these decisions, taken in connection with those of the state courts, corresponds to the general trend over the United States, the extreme points reached being that at which the wearing of distinctive religious garb is held to constitute sectarian instruction or influence, and that at which the excusing of pupils by school officials to obtain outside religious instruction is declared unconstitutional and illegal by one jurisdiction of the

Appellate branch of the Supreme Court and declared constitutional and legal by another jurisdiction of the same Court.

Table I gives a summary of findings gathered from the detailed analysis of twenty-five cases selected from the total of forty-five cases that are the source of the data for this chapter. There are nineteen states represented in this collection of cases. At least one case from each state is included in Table I. In this collection of forty-five cases there are eleven states represented by a single case, five states represented by two cases, two states represented by three cases, and one state, New York, represented by eighteen cases. Of these eighteen cases from New York only three are from the state's higher courts proper, the other fifteen being decisions by the State Superintendent or State Commissioner of Education.

The remaining twenty cases are discussed in greater or less detail under the proper state heading. There were various reasons why these cases were not summarized in Table I. The omitted California case has but slight connection with the subject of the chapter and could be best presented by discussion. The same is true of one of the two Illinois cases omitted, while the other was decided on a technical point of pleading. Only one of the cases decided by the Commissioner of Education of New York is included in Table I; namely, the latest case on the issue. The others are discussed briefly. The latest New York court case was omitted because no official report of it was in print at the time this study was written. It also was similar to one of the New York court cases included. One Ohio case was omitted because it was a case from a court of inferior jurisdiction and followed the decision in the Ohio case included. One Wisconsin case was omitted because the Supreme Court held that the issues really pertinent to this study were not presented by the appeal to that Court. However, these cases were considered in developing the remainder of the summary.

SUMMARY OF FINDINGS NOT INCLUDED IN TABLE I

I. Constitutional and Statutory Provisions:

1. No very definite statement can be made as to the constitutionality or legality of the various manifestations of the

religious impulse displayed in the public schools. Historical background as well as constitutional and statutory provisions vary so much that each manifestation must be judged from the viewpoint of the state in which it occurs. The following statements seem to be as definite as conditions warrant one in making:

    a. Public school funds or property may not be used in aid or support of sectarian organizations or purposes.

    b. Every pupil has the right to enjoy the opportunities provided in the public schools without restraint or hindrance to his freedom of worship and liberty of conscience.

    c. It is the policy of the states that public schools shall not be influenced, directly or indirectly, by sectarian organizations or practices.

II. Excusing Pupils from School to Attend Religious Instruction:

1. It will take a decision by the New York Court of Appeals to determine the constitutionality and the legality of excusing pupils at the request of parents for the purpose of attending upon outside religious instruction, since there are two courts of inferior but equal rank holding opposite views.

III. The State and Religion:

1. The Michigan and Ohio Supreme Courts have held that the Ordinance of 1787 now has no effect in placing those states under any duty or obligation to teach religion.

2. The Washington and Illinois Supreme Courts have taken the position that the constitutions of those states were designed to prohibit any religious exercise, recognition, or influence in the public schools.

3. The Georgia Supreme Court has taken the position that there is evidence that Georgia had never intended to require the separation of State and religion; that it is not the policy of the State to be unreligious or unchristian. The Georgia Court shows how the State is still affected by its early connection between Church and State.

IV. Criteria for Determining a Sectarian Book:

1. The California and Kentucky Supreme Courts isolated the following criteria for determining whether a book is sectarian:

a. The book itself must show that it teaches the peculiar dogma of a sect as such and not alone that it is comprehensive enough to include them by the partial interpretation of its adherents.

b. It is the character and the contents of the book that determine whether or not it is sectarian.

c. The authorship of the book is not a test nor is the church membership of the author a test.

d. The use to which the book is put does not make it sectarian.

e. The extent of approval by different sects does not determine it.

f. That a book is commonly adopted or believed to be inspired by one sect does not make it a sectarian book.

g. Sectarian instruction is that which inculcates doctrines or dogma concerning which the religious sects are in conflict.

V. Bible Reading, Prayers, and the Like:

1. Bible reading, unaccompanied by other practices, occurred in only three of the cases studied.

2. The constitutionality of a statute forbidding the exclusion of the Bible from the public schools was upheld by the Iowa Supreme Court in 1884.

3. The Supreme Court of Texas has taken the position that "one or more" dissenters have not the right to use the courts to prohibit the great majority from having their children instructed through Bible reading.

4. The Louisiana Supreme Court has held that Bible reading and the recital of the Lord's Prayer as school exercises constitute a preference to Christian pupils as against Jews.

5. The Supreme Courts of Wisconsin and Louisiana have expressed the opinion that the excusing of pupils from Bible reading, prayer, etc., does not help to make the exercises constitutional but is rather an admission of the force of the objections to the practice.

6. "Selections from the Bible" as a book of material for Bible reading was upheld by the Michigan Supreme Court.

7. The holding of the Supreme Courts of Ohio, Nebraska, and Iowa, that Bible reading might be had in the public schools at

the option of the local officials, was not a denial of the legislature's power to control the prescription of studies for the schools.

8. The Supreme Court of Maine in 1854 held that a school board might expel a pupil for refusing to read from the King James version of the Bible, the regularly adopted textbook in reading.

9. While holding that the Bible as a whole might not be read in the public schools, the Wisconsin Supreme Court expressed the opinion that much of the Bible might properly be used for secular instruction.

10. Bible reading, prayers, and hymns have been held by the highest courts (1) to convert the school into a "place of worship" by Nebraska and Wisconsin and not so by Iowa, Kentucky, Texas, and Michigan; (2) to make the teacher a "minister of religion" by Wisconsin and not so by Kentucky, Texas, and Michigan; (3) not to convert the school into a "religious seminary" by Texas and Michigan.

VI. General Religion:

1. While some of the decisions have supported "general religion," "natural religion," etc., no court has drawn a sharp line of distinction either between general religious instruction and sectarian instruction, or between religious worship and Bible reading or secular Bible study.

VII. The Pennsylvania Supreme Court has held that the exclusion of a "Sister of Charity" from teaching because she was a Catholic would be a violation of the spirit of the state constitution.

VIII. The constitutionality of a statute forbidding the wearing of distinctive religious garb by a teacher in the schoolroom has been upheld by the Pennsylvania Supreme Court.

IX. The Supreme Courts of North Dakota and Iowa and the New York Commissioner of Education have held that it is contrary to the policy of the state to arrange to hold a public school in a sectarian building indefinitely.

X. The California Supreme Court in 1921 held that requiring pupils to participate in dancing at school against the parents' objections on the ground of religious scruples was a violation of the constitutions of the United States and the State.

XI. The Supreme Courts of Maine and Vermont and the Commissioner of Education of New York have held that conscientious belief that a school law or regulation is wrong will not excuse the disobeying of such law or regulation.

CHAPTER VI

JUDICIAL DECISIONS RELATING TO THE MATTER OF INSTRUCTIONAL SUPPLIES IN THE PUBLIC SCHOOLS

The kind of instructional supplies that are available for instructing the children and the matter of the agencies purchasing and paying for them are elements of curriculum control that have been greatly affected by the decisions of the courts of our country. Free instructional supplies may be made available for the instruction of the children of the public schools through either one or both of the following agencies: (1) The local school corporation may furnish such supplies, pursuant to statutory provisions, either upon the initiative of the local school officials or upon the initiative and vote of the electors of the local district. (2) The state, authorized by legislative enactment, may furnish instructional supplies at the expense of the state or may require the local school corporations to provide such supplies. It is important that those who are interested in the curriculum of the public schools may know what attitude our courts have taken upon the issues relating to the providing of instructional supplies for our schools. In this part of the study only those cases have been considered whose issues relate to what the supplies may be or how they may be provided.

THE FURNISHING OF GENERAL INSTRUCTIONAL EQUIPMENT

For the purposes of this study "general instructional equipment" is considered as including such equipment as meets the conditions set up in the following quotation from the Indiana Supreme Court: [1]

Blackboards, charts, maps, tellurians, and dictionaries are a class of articles, apparatus and books which are not required for each individual scholar, but one of each would be sufficient, in most instances, for the whole school, and would be used by the teacher in giving instruction to the pupils. No person being required to furnish such common property for the benefit of the whole school, they can only be supplied by the trustee.

Must the Purchases Be Authorized by the Electors of the District? The early tendency to keep the control of the expenditures of the school district's funds in the hands of the voters of the district is shown by several decisions upholding statutes that required that the expenditures for general instructional equipment be directly passed upon by the voters or at least be authorized by them. The Supreme Courts of Arkansas [2] in 1910 and Ohio [3] in 1894 gave such decisions.

The trend toward allowing the trustees of the school corporations to initiate and control the expenditures for "general instructional equipment" is plainly shown by lines of cases in Michigan and Iowa. In each of these states the supreme court was called upon early to decide cases which necessitated the construction of statutes that prohibited the purchase by a school director of any charts or apparatus for the school without having already had the vote of the district electors authorizing the same. The Iowa Court [4] in 1868 upheld such a statute.

In 1876 the Iowa Supreme Court [5] held that, since there was a statute which provided that school boards might "use any unappropriated contingent fund in the treasury to purchase records, dictionaries, maps, charts, and apparatus for the use of the schools of their districts"; since the district at its annual meeting had exercised its statutory power in determining that music should be taught in its schools; since a musical instrument is properly connected with a musical education so as to be denominated "apparatus"; since nothing is shown to the contrary, it is to be presumed that there were "unappropriated contingent funds" on hand; therefore, the school board might contract for the purchase of an organ to be paid for out of any "unappropriated funds."

In 1890 the Iowa Court [6] held that a new statute, which provided that physiology and hygiene should be taught and which made it the duty of the school board to make provision for the observance of the act upon penalty of forfeiting their proportion of the school fund for failure to do so, did not exclude the operation of the statute concerning "unappropriated funds" as men-

tioned in the case [5] above. This Court also held that purchases
under the provisions of that law [5] must be made with cash
actually in the treasury at the time of the contract and
"unappropriated." The Court further held that the board could
not take funds that would in the usual course of carrying on the
schools be used for such things as fuel, salaries of the board, etc.,
and use them for the purchase of charts, apparatus, etc., and then
have the voters at the next annual meeting appropriate funds for
such fuel and salary bills. It was the theory of the Court that
all of the available contingent fund that was necessary to meet
these annual, regular, operating expenses had been "appropriated" at the beginning of the year.

Later another statute put the entire control of the district
schools into the hands of the board of township directors. One
such board purchased some sets of mathematical blocks for the
schools. The director in charge of one school refused to allow
this apparatus to be placed in his school on the grounds that the
apparatus was worthless and its purchase illegal. The Court
[7] held that the board had entire control of the schools; that
the subdirector had no right to forbid the use of the apparatus
which had been legally purchased; that an injunction would lie
against him to prevent his interfering.

In Michigan one early statute forbade the purchase by a school
director of any charts or apparatus for the school without the
previous vote of the district authorizing the same. Another
statute made it the duty of the director to provide necessary
"appendages" for the schoolhouse. Directors attempted to buy
all sorts of supplies for the school under the latter act without
the authorization of the voters. It is very interesting to note that
the Michigan cases present an almost exact duplication of the
Iowa cases just discussed. In Michigan the cases turned upon
what was included in the term "necessary appendages for a
schoolhouse."

In 1877 the Michigan Court [8] held that school charts are not
such "necessary appendages." In 1885 the same Court [9]
explained:

The word "appendage," as used in our school statutes, does not
mean simply the school apparatus to be used inside the building; nor
do I think it can be limited to such articles as brooms, pails, cups, etc.

but must be construed in a broader sense, as it has been in other courts, to include fuel, fences, and necessary out-buildings.

By 1887 a special study had been introduced into the curriculum and the Michigan Court [10] decided that the board of trustees of a graded school had authority to purchase a piano for a high school where music was one of the subjects taught. The Michigan Court [11] swung back toward its early conservatism when it decided that a new statute, which provided that the directors should introduce physiology and hygiene and select a textbook therefor, did not alter the older law which required the district's vote

. . . to allow the purchase of a certain book (Yaggy's Anatomical Chart) containing plates, etc., which, however convenient in the study, is still not needed to give the law effect.

This unusual parallelism of statutes and cases is continued in the Michigan statute of 1921 and a case [12] construing it in 1923. The statute of 1921 gave school district boards authority to vote taxes

for regular running expenses of the schools which shall include school furnishings and all appurtenances, the care of school property, teachers' wages, water supply, premium upon indemnity bond for the treasurer of the district, transportation of pupils, record books and blanks, and all apparatus and material which may be necessary in order that the schools may be properly managed and maintained.

In spite of this clear and explicit law a case was carried to the Supreme Court involving the right of the district board to purchase apparatus and material without the previous authorization of the voters. The Court in upholding this right for the district board said:

It was manifestly the intent of the legislature that the district board should see that the school property was maintained in a usable condition and supplied with all the apparatus and material necessary to the proper conduct of the school.

The cases [18, 22, 24] reported from other states imply that the local school officials have power to purchase "general instructional equipment" upon their own initiative, at least up to a certain maximum amount per year.

What General Instructional Equipment May Be Furnished?
The cases involving this issue have usually arisen when school
trustees sought to buy for the general use of the schools such
articles as maps, charts, globes, musical instruments, dictionaries,
stereoscopes and views, mathematical blocks, etc., under the
authority of statutes which have used such general terms as
"make provision for," "appendages," "apparatus," "furnish,"
"furniture," "running expenses," "appliances," etc., in designating
the things which the trustees of local school corporations might
provide for general use in the schools. The discussion of the Iowa
and Michigan cases supra shows the trend in each state from the
point in the first case [4 and 8] where the Court held that the
board of directors had absolutely no power to purchase maps,
charts, globes, etc., without a previous vote of the electors authorizing their action, to a point in the second case [5 and 9] in each
line of cases where the Court decreed that, since the board had
been authorized to add music to the curriculum, it might, therefore, purchase a musical instrument with which to teach music.
In each state the next step involved the effect of the passage of
another statute, which required the teaching of physiology and
hygiene and "making provisions therefor," upon the earlier
statute which provided that the district school board might not
purchase maps, charts, etc., without the previous vote of the
electors. The Courts of both states held that the early statute
was not affected by the new statute, thus restricting the power of
the boards. The final step gave the local officials complete control of such purchases.

The Indiana cases show a different development. There the
question of authorization by the district voters never came before
the court. In 1877 the Supreme Court [13] held that as a dic-
tionary was for general use and not for the use of one particular
pupil, and as it was necessary for the successful work of the
school, the trustee might purchase such books for the schools.
By 1885 the Indiana statutes were beginning to safeguard the
school corporations by restricting the right of the trustees to
incur school indebtedness entirely at their own discretion, but
the Supreme Court [14] in that year held as follows:

The statutes relating to the power of trustees to incur indebtedness
have no application to the ordinary debts incurred by a trustee for
supplies (globes in this case) for the schools of his township.

The statement of the Indiana Court [1] has been quoted supra in giving the idea as to what was included in the term "general instructional supplies." The Indiana Appellate Court [15] in 1901 stated that under the statutes then existing school trustees had authority to prescribe the teaching of music in the common schools and that this carried with it the authority to purchase music charts for the purpose of the general instruction of pupils, although music was not one of the subjects prescribed by the legislature for the public schools. A trend toward sound budgetary procedure—as well as the court's attitude upon the trustee's power to purchase supplies—can be seen in the decision of the Indiana Appellate Court [16] in 1903. It declared that, under the statute which had created an advisory board to the township trustee and which had specified that the trustee might not create a debt not embraced in the annual estimates, without special authority given him by the advisory board, there could be no recovery by a vendor on a trustee's contract for apparatus made without authority from the advisory board.

The Kansas Supreme Court [17] in 1879 decided that a stereoscope and stereoscopic views were not "necessary appendages" for the schoolhouse, within the meaning of the statute which prescribed what the district board should provide. In 1883 the same court [18] held that a mathematical chart might be deemed either an "apparatus" or an "appendage" within the meaning of those terms in the statutes which conferred upon school district boards the authority to make purchases for school purposes. A different phase of this "general instructional equipment" question is presented by the decision of the Kansas Supreme Court [19] in 1913. The Court decided that a contract between the state school textbook commission and the author of a primary reading chart to supply the needs of the state therefor, did not compel a school district board to purchase one of the charts for a district school, under the statutes relating to the purchase of charts, maps, and other appendages.

The Ohio Supreme Court [3] in 1894 held that a "Tellurian Globe" is an "appendage" within the meaning of the statute which limits the amount which a board of education may expend for such purposes in one year. This case was followed by the same Court [20] in 1900.

In 1890 the New York State Superintendent [21] upheld the

right of the director of a school district to reimbursement to the amount of $15.00 per year for charts which he had bought without the vote of the district.

The Texas Court of Appeals [22] in 1897 decided that a statute which authorized school trustees to buy "furniture" for schoolhouses did not authorize the purchase of a "Normal Series Grammar Chart."

The West Virginia Supreme Court [23] in 1896 upheld the purchase of maps, charts, etc., and made this statement:

. . . It must be made to appear that they (charts, maps, etc.) are not mere school books in some other form or under some other name, but something of which a few will answer the needs of all, suitable to the school, and reasonably necessary to enable the teacher to impart instruction to the pupils more efficiently in such branches as are required to be taught.

THE PROVISION OF FREE INDIVIDUAL EQUIPMENT

Textbooks. The power of the legislature to pass legislation providing that the state shall furnish free textbooks to the children of the common schools, or that the local school corporations shall furnish such free textbooks, has rarely been questioned. California is the only state where a case has been found in which the legislature's right to require that free textbooks be furnished to any of the children has been challenged. In 1912 the California constitution was amended so as to provide that free textbooks and supplies should be furnished for the use of the children in the elementary school. In 1917 the legislature passed an act which provided for free textbooks for high school pupils. A suit was brought to mandate the State Board of Education and the State Superintendent to issue a list of high school textbooks in conformity with the Free Book Law. The Supreme Court [24] held that, while there was no direct constitutional provision for free textbooks for high schools, no further authority was needed for supplying free textbooks for such schools at the discretion of the legislature than the general powers granted by the constitution under which the high school system itself had been created, operated, and maintained; that there was nothing in the constitutional requirement for free textbooks for elementary schools which negatived a legislative power also to supply such books to secondary schools; that there was nothing in the nature of a

provision for free textbooks for high schools to require different
or more specific constitutional authority than had been found
sufficient for the building and furnishing of schoolhouses, employing teachers, and supplying high school equipment including
pens, charts, etc.

This Court also held that the furnishing of free textbooks to
high school students was not a gift that came within the prohibition of the constitution because it was simply carrrying out the
constitutional requirement for furnishing free schools and encour-
aging learning. It held that this was particularly true in view of
the fact that the free school system is not primarily a service to
individuals, but to the state and for the state's own welfare. The
Court also held that such a provision by the legislature was not
unconstitutional in the sense that it was an attempt to impose
taxes upon a high school district by direct legislative action and
without the interposition of the regularly constituted taxing
officials.

Concerning the power of local school boards to furnish free
textbooks without the authorization of a state statute, the Michigan Supreme Court [25] expressed itself as follows in 1890:

It has never been claimed, so far as we are aware, that school boards
have the power to furnish free .textbooks except by virtue of special
legislation.

In this case the board of education of Detroit had attempted to
furnish free textbooks simply by including in its annual estimate
a sum for free textbooks. In announcing its decision the Court
said that such action, in the absence of authority from a majority
of the qualified electors as provided by statute, was absolutely
void.

This matter of furnishing free textbooks without the authorization of legislative enactment is found to have been raised at least
twice in courts of inferior jurisdiction in Pennsylvania before
1890. A County Court [26] in 1882 held that the statutes
authorizing boards of education to provide suitable books for
"indigent blind children" and to pay for them out of the school
fund "as in the case of seeing children," did not authorize the
board to furnish free books for all school children and to pay the
salary of a librarian. Here was a plain case of an attempt to
stretch the law, which had been passed to provide for poor chil-

dren and which had been amended by a law which was passed to
provide suitable books for blind children, and to take advantage
of the phrase "as in the case of seeing children" in a way entirely
unwarranted.

It is very interesting to note the position taken in 1883 by
another Pennsylvania court of inferior jurisdiction on this matter
of free textbooks. The Chester County Court [27] stated its
position thus:

> The acts authorizing school directors to direct what branches of
> learning shall be taught in each school and what books shall be used,
> authorize school directors to purchase and pay for school books which
> have been selected by them according to law for the use of the children
> of the district. . . . This power is not given by the express terms of
> any statute, but is to be deduced from the general powers granted to
> directors of schools by the common laws. Nor is express authority
> given to the directors to purchase maps, globes, blackboards, etc., yet,
> it is evidently intended the directors shall pay for them. . . . The
> school system provided by the earlier statutes was limited to such
> schools as "that the poor might be taught gratis"; the present system
> contemplates the education of all children without distinction. To
> carry out the liberal purposes intended by our present system, all
> necessary means must be employed.

The Iowa Supreme Court [28] in 1905 held that:

> The maintenance of public schools does not necessarily involve the
> furnishing of school books to scholars; nor can it be implied from the
> authority to maintain schools that a school board may compel tax-
> payers in general, regardless of whether they have children attending
> the schools, to pay taxes for the purpose not only of supporting schools,
> but of enabling the children who attend them to have books without
> cost, or at a lower cost than that at which the books can be procured
> without the expenditure of public money.

The Illinois Appellate Court [29] decided this question in the
same way when the board of education of a city attempted to
supply free textbooks to all the children of the first four grades
of the city schools without reference to whether parents were able
to furnish such books.

In Washington a school board attempted to disregard the vote
of the district which favored the furnishing of free textbooks for
the high school as well as the elementary school, the vote having
been taken in accordance with the statutory provisions. The

Supreme Court [30] held that the law left no discretion with the board and that it might be mandated to furnish free textbooks to all.

The New York Commissioner held in 1923 [31], that, where the statute provided that the vote of a district meeting on the issue of furnishing free textbooks should be taken by recording the ayes and noes and the meeting voted by ballot in favor of free textbooks, the vote would be set aside.

Free Textbooks to Children of Parochial School. An interesting question arose as late as 1922 from the practice of a New York public school corporation which furnished free textbooks to all the children who were attending schools in the city, parochial schools included. In this case [32] the Supreme Court held that free textbooks were issued to the public school corporation and not to the individual children; that the furnishing of free school books and supplies to children attending other than the public schools was not authorized by law and was in contravention of the constitution of New York which provides that:

> Neither the state nor any subdivision thereof shall use its property or credit, or any public money directly or indirectly in aid or maintenance, other than for examination or inspection, of any school or institution of learning wholly or in part under the control or direction of any religious denomination, or in which any denominational doctrine or tenet is taught.

Free Supplementary Books. Indiana, Michigan, Kansas, and Washington are the only states in which cases have been found that raise the issue of the power of the local school corporation to furnish free supplementary books. The Indiana Supreme Court [1] in 1889 upheld the power of the trustee to purchase "general instructional equipment" but was very emphatic in saying that:

> The authority, certainly, cannot be extended to the right of purchasing general textbooks for the use of each of the individual pupils.

The right of a township trustee to buy "reading-circle books" was an issue before the Indiana Appellate Court [33] in 1896. The Court here held that a township trustee, under his statutory authority "to provide suitable furniture, apparatus, and other articles and educational appliances necessary for the thorough organization and efficient management" of the schools of his township, could not buy "reading-circle books" and render the township liable therefor. In the next case a township trustee had attempted to purchase a "reading-circle library and cases" under the provisions of a statute authorizing trustees "to provide suitable houses, furniture, apparatus, and other articles and educational appliances necessary for schools." The Appellate Court [34] held that the trustee had no such authority and that a warrant, stating that it was given for such articles, was void on its face.

In Michigan where a board of education passed a resolution to purchase certain textbooks for "supplementary use" in the schools, the Supreme Court [35] in 1903 decided that, since there was no intention of adopting the books within the sense of the statute concerning the adoption of textbooks, the purchase of books in consequence of the resolution was illegal and void.

This issue arose in Washington where a board of education prescribed a course of study which required that the textbooks adopted by the state be "supplemented" by the use of other books on the same subject. The Supreme Court [36] decided that such a course of study was inconsistent with the law of the state and not authorized by the school code which gave such directors the power to grade the school.

In Kansas the Department of Public Instruction had construed the textbook law as permitting the use of supplementary readers, provided the regularly adopted books were also used in good faith. The State Department had also stated in its course of study that, unless supplementary readers could be used, the work of the schools would be much hampered. A school city had adopted certain supplementary readers to be used in connection with the readers adopted by the State Textbook Commission. An injunction was asked against such use in 1913. The lower court held that to enjoin the use of such supplementary readers would be "most harmful to the school children and a most unconscionable exercise of the equity powers of the court." The attitude of the Supreme Court [37] is shown by its decision that the uniformity act required the use of the same textbooks in all the schools, in order to lessen the expense while insuring the quality; that the board of education had no power to adopt and use in its schools other books than those adopted by the state, except such "proper books of reference" as might reasonably be used as such.

The theory of the court in this case was that the State Board of Education should not be allowed to exercise a power which really amounted to amending the law, so as to control the action of the State Textbook Commission; that a statute which had been passed in 1897 and which stated that no board of education should allow any teacher to exclude as a "basic textbook" any textbook adopted by the State Textbook Commission did not show any intention of amending the uniform textbook law. However, the real feeling and attitude of this Court is no doubt made clear by the following quotation from the last page of the decision:

No more insidious and yet effective manner of nullifying the statute and bringing back the very burden it was intended to dissipate could well be devised than the one used in this case. If obedience to the law, as it now exists, works harm to certain pupils who complete the use of the adopted readers before the close of the term, the legislative and not the judicial department is the one to enact needed amendments.

The legislature's power to compel school districts to purchase a particular book and to withhold from the district's portion of the state common school fund the price of the book was tested in a Kentucky case [38]. The act provided that, if at the annual district election for school trustees the electors did not by vote decide not to purchase a copy of "Collins's Historical Sketches of Kentucky" and if the district did not certify this vote officially to the State Superintendent before a certain date, then the Superintendent should purchase a copy for that district and the price should be withheld from the state fund due that district. The Court of Appeals upheld that part of the law which required the book to be bought for the district but it declared unconstitutional that part of it which provided that the price of the book should be withheld from the common school fund due the district as that fund was inviolable.

Instructional Equipment Other Than Textbooks. In 1884 an Ohio court of inferior jurisdiction [39] held that a board of education had no authority to purchase material such as copy books, ink, paper, pens, pencils, etc., for free distribution to pupils without regard to the ability of their parents to provide such material. It seems rather strange that no court of final jurisdiction has ever been called upon to decide this question. It is well known that boards of education do furnish such materials in varying proportions in many of the states.

The courts have persistently supported statutes that have attempted to prevent school board members assuming any relations in the sale of textbooks and supplies that might lead to charges of misuse of their official position. Such situations might easily lead to the adoption of inferior textbooks and instructional supplies.

The Iowa Supreme Court in 1905 upheld a statute which provided that the directors of a public school might adopt textbooks, contract for and buy and sell the same at cost—the proceeds of sales to be turned into the contingent fund—and that they might select persons to keep such adopted books for sale. However, the Court [28] held:

A board has no right to contract with a book-seller to sell books to scholars at cost in consideration of payments to be made to him out of the contingent fund of the district.

In 1906 the Iowa Supreme Court [40] decided that the statutes prohibited any school director from acting in any way as agent or dealer in school textbooks and supplies.

The West Virginia Supreme Court [41] in 1904 decided that a contract made by a member of a board of education for the sale, to another school board, of articles for use in a free school was void under the statute.

The Michigan Supreme Court [42] in 1913 decided that a city board of education had no authority, either under any statute or independent of it, to purchase high school books for the purpose of reselling them to pupils at cost.

The Wisconsin Supreme Court [43] in 1914 held that a school board had no authority under the statute to authorize high school principals to conduct stores in the school buildings for the sale of books and supplies at a personal profit.

The Texas Court of Appeals [44] in 1916 decided that the acts of the principal, superintendent, and school trustees in starting a school cafeteria and supply house and punishing pupils who purchased supplies elsewhere amounted to a boycott and so was beyond their authority.

TREND OF THE DECISIONS

1. The trend of the decisions shows a departure from the early practice of requiring that all purchases of "general instructional equipment" be authorized by the previous vote of the electors of the district toward the practice of giving the local officials full control of such matters.

a. The decisions show a trend toward approval of the requirement that such purchases be provided for in an annual estimate to be presented by the purchasing officials to the electors or an advisory board.

2. There is a decided trend in the decisions towards being increasingly liberal in construing the statutory powers of school officials in purchasing whatever general instructional equipment the best interests of the children of the schools demand.

SUMMARY

I. The higher courts have been very liberal on the whole in construing the statutory powers of local school corporations to furnish whatever "general instructional equipment" was necessary for the efficient conduct of the public schools.

II. The higher courts have been very liberal in construing the statutory powers of local school corporation officials to purchase "general educational equipment" without the previous specific authorization of the voters of the district, while upholding the practice of including such material in annual estimates or budgets.

III. The higher courts have always taken the position that the state, through the legislative department, has the power to provide free textbooks for the public schools.

IV. The following principles have been set up regarding the furnishing of free textbooks to the public schools:

1. Specific legislative authority is necessary.

2. Free textbooks may be furnished to high schools as well as to the elementary schools.

3. When statutory requirements have been met there is no discretion left to the local board as to furnishing free textbooks.

4. Free textbooks are furnished to the public school corporations and not to individual children. Attendance upon a public

school is a prerequisite to the right to the use of a free textbook.

5. The courts have construed the laws strictly against the furnishing of free textbooks "supplementing regularly adopted textbooks."

V. The courts of final jurisdiction have not been asked to pass upon the power of local school corporations to furnish free individual equipment other than textbooks.

VI. The courts have interpreted very strictly, as against school officials, the rights and powers of such officials in assuming the relations of agent for or vendor of school supplies.

CITATIONS ON CHAPTER VI

1. Honey Creek School Township v. Barnes, 119 Ind. 213.
2. First National Bank v. Whisenhunt, 94 Ark. 583.
3. Board of Education v. Andrews, 51 Ohio St. 199.
4. Taylor v. District of Otter Creek, 26 Iowa 281.
5. Bellmeyer v. Independent District of Marshalltown, 44 Iowa 564.
6. Yaggy v. District Township of Monroe, 80 Iowa 121.
7. District v. Meyers, 83 Ia. 688.
8. Gibson v. School District No. 5, 36 Mich. 404.
9. Greager v. School District, 62 Mich. 101.
10. Knabe v. Board of Education West Bay City, 67 Mich. 262.
11. Western Publishing House v. School District No. 1, 94 Mich. 262.
12. Commercial State Bank v. School District No. 3, 196 N. W. (Mich.) 373.
13. Jackson v. Hadley, 59 Ind. 534.
14. Miller v. White River School Township, 101 Ind. 503.
15. Myers Publishing Co. v. White River School Township, 28 Ind. App. 91.
16. Lincoln Township v. American School Furniture Co., 31 Ind. App. 405.
    Union National Bank v. Franklin School Township, 31 Ind. App. 699.
17. School District No. 9 v. Perkins, 21 Kan. 536.
18. School District No. 17 v. Swayze, 29 Kan. 211.
19. Pendry v. Edgar, 88 Kan. 830.
20. Board of Education Harrison Township v. First Nat. Bank, 61 Ohio St. 666.
21. Finegan, Decisions New York Supt. 767.
22. McGee v. Franklin Publishing Co., 15 Texas Civ. App. 216.
23. Hanaker v. Board of Education, 42 W. Va. 170.
24. Macmillan Company v. Clarke, 184 Cal. 491.
25. Board of Education v. Common Council Detroit, 80 Mich. 548.
26. 12 Weekly Notes Cases 125, Pa.
27. Wickersham's Appeal, 1 Chester County Reports 509, Pa.
28. Reis v. Hemmer, 127 Iowa 408.
29. Harris v. Kill, 108 Ill. App. 305.

30. Hand v. School District No. 1, 118 Wash. 439.
31. 30 New York State Dept. Rep. 140.
32. Smith v. Donahue, 195 N. Y. S. 715.
33. First National Bank v. Adams School Township, 17 Ind. App. 375.
34. First National Bank v. Osborne, 18 Ind. App. 442.
35. Attorney General ex rel. Marr v. Board of Education, 133 Mich. 681.
36. Westland Publishing Company v. Royal, 36 Wash. 399.
37. State of Kansas ex rel. Dawson v. Innes, 89 Kan. 168.
38. Collins v. Henderson, 74 Ky. 74.
39. Parker v. Board of Education of Cleveland, 9 Ohio Decisions 335.
40. State of Iowa v. Wick, 130 Iowa 31.
41. Poling v. Board of Education, 56 W. Va. 251.
42. Attorney General ex rel. Sheehan v. Board of Ed. Detroit, 175 Mich. 438.
43. Tyre v. Krug, 159 Wis. 39.
44. Hailey v. Brooks, 191 S. W. (Tex.) 781.

CHAPTER VII

JUDICIAL DECISIONS RELATING TO THE ADOPTION AND CHANGE OF TEXTBOOKS IN THE PUBLIC SCHOOLS

Who has the power to adopt textbooks? How are they adopted? How may adopted textbooks be changed? These issues indirectly affect the curriculum of the public common schools. The courts are often called upon to decide questions involving these issues. It is not considered to be the purpose of this study to go into a detailed study and analysis of all the cases that in any way involve the adoption of textbooks, the contracting for them, and their change. That in itself offers a field for a separate study. Cases which involve only the procedure and machinery of adoption or change of textbooks have not been considered. Nor have those cases in which the issues are purely issues concerning the law of contracts been discussed. It does not follow that a case is pertinent to this study simply because the contract upon which the case is based is a contract for textbooks. It is the intention in this chapter merely to bring out those underlying principles concerning the adoption and change of textbooks that seem most likely to affect the curriculum.

No cases have been found in this study in which the content of a textbook was attacked, other than those cases dealing with the Bible. Those cases were discussed in Chapter V.

WHAT ARE UNIFORM TEXTBOOKS?

Some decisions have been found in which the court had this issue before it. The liberality of the court in construing a statute in which the term "textbooks" and "school supplies" were used is apparent in the following quotation from a decision of the Nebraska Supreme Court [1] in 1917:

The general question is whether the words "school supplies," found in the tenth section of the act, is embraced within the meaning of the term "textbooks." "School supplies," as used in this act, means maps, globes, and other apparatus necessary for use in schools, and we think that a chart or a map or a globe is as much a textbook as a reader or speller, within the purposes and intention of the act under consideration. We do not think that the term "textbooks" should be given a technical meaning, but that it is comprehensive enough to and does include globes, maps, charts, pens, ink, paper, etc., and all other apparatus and appliances which are proper to be used in the schools in instructing the youth; and we conclude, therefore, that the act under consideration is not broader than its title, and that the term "school supplies," found in the tenth section of the act, is not foreign to the term "textbooks" found in the title of the act, but is germane to, and comprehended and included within the term "textbooks."

Further light is thrown upon the attitude of the courts in defining the term "textbooks" by noting that the Illinois Supreme Court [2] in 1898 and the New York State Superintendent [3] in 1888 held that writing-books were textbooks under the statutes of their respective states.

The Michigan Supreme Court [4] in 1903 made the following statement concerning "uniformity" of textbooks:

The term "uniformity" does not mean that all the textbooks of one author in grammar, arithmetic, history, physiology, etc., for the different grades of scholars must be used. Boards of education are at liberty, under this law, to adopt the book of one author for use in all the primary departments, and the book of another author on the same subject in all the grammar or higher departments. All the law requires is that they be uniform in the same grade.

In 1912 the Kansas Supreme Court [5] expressed its interpretation of the term "uniform series" of textbooks as follows:

We construe the words "uniform series" to mean the whole series adopted for use in the schools. Their use must be uniform in all the schools of the grade where the particular book is used. The intent of the legislature was not to provide a set of books on one subject necessarily by the same author. When a series of readers has been adopted it may be made up of books prepared by different authors. It is no less a uniform series of readers if the reader adopted for use in each grade is by a different author.

THE NECESSITY FOR A UNIFORM SERIES OF TEXTBOOKS

Must a state have a uniform series of textbooks adopted and in use in its schools in order to fulfill the usual constitutional

requirement that the legislature shall provide a "uniform system
of common schools"? This question has been answered by the
courts of a number of states [6] and the general attitude of the
courts seems to have been well expressed by the Montana Supreme Court [7] in 1896 as follows:

We do not think the clause in the Constitution quoted above requires
the adoption of a uniform series of textbooks throughout the State
by that body (the Legislature). We think the duty of establishing
and maintaining "a general, uniform, and thorough system of public,
free, common schools" imposed by the constitution upon the legislative assembly, does not necessarily imply that that body shall establish
and maintain a uniform series of textbooks throughout the state for use
in the public schools. The states of Minnesota, Indiana, Washington,
Mississippi, Kansas, Wisconsin, and Illinois have constitutional provisions very similar to ours in relation to public schools. In none of
these states has it ever been considered, either by the legislature or
courts, that the constitutional provision requiring the legislature to
establish and maintain a uniform system of free common schools made
it necessary that the textbooks used in the schools should be uniform
throughout the state, in order that there should be a uniform system of
schools.

THE ADOPTION OF TEXTBOOKS

Who Has the Power Over the Adoption of Textbooks?

The Indiana Supreme Court [8] in 1889 made a very clear
and emphatic statement concerning the power of the legislative
department of the government over this matter. The Court said
in part:

Both by the constitution and by the intrinsic nature of the duty and
the power, the authority (over the schools) is exclusively legislative,
and the matter over which it is to be exercised solely a matter of state
concern. . . . No case has been cited by counsel, and none has been
discovered by us, although we have searched the reports with care,
which denies the doctrine that the regulation of the public schools is
a state matter exclusively within the domain of the legislature. . . .
It is impossible to conceive of the existence of a uniform system of
common schools without power lodged somewhere to make it uniform,
and, even in the absence of express constitutional provisions, that
power must necessarily reside in the legislature. If it does reside there,
then that body must have, as an incident of the principal power, the
authority to prescribe the course of study and the system of instruction that shall be pursued and adopted, as well as *the books which
shall be used.*

The location of the power to adopt textbooks in California in 1880 is explained by the following excerpt from a decision of the Supreme Court [9] handed down in that year:

> The new constitution, which is, of course, above the statute, says that the "local boards" shall adopt a series of textbooks. Here, then, clearly seems to be a power given. It does not say "in such manner as the legislature may prescribe," but the local board "shall adopt." . . . Possibly the legislature may prescribe rules by which boards shall be governed in selecting books . . . but such legislation could not be used to take away the right of ultimate selection.

This is a good example of the power of the sovereign people to control a matter, which as a general rule [10 and 11] seems to be accepted as falling within the powers of the legislature of the state, by putting an explicit provision in the constitution to govern it. This case furnishes the only exception to the general position on this matter that has been found in this study.

The right of the legislature to make special provisions concerning the adoption of textbooks was upheld by the Minnesota Supreme Court [12] in 1911. The Court decided that the city of St. Paul was not bound by a general statute which provided that adopted textbooks might not be changed within three years from the date of their adoption. It was explained by the Court that the provisions of the statute conflicted with the provisions of a special charter granted previously by the legislature to the city of St. Paul.

The Supreme Courts [13] of Indiana, Nebraska, and Michigan have held that whenever local school corporations are permitted by the statute to determine that branches of learning, in addition to those prescribed by the statutes, may be prescribed for their local schools, then the local corporation has the right to adopt textbooks for such subjects as it adds to its curriculum.

The Appellate and Supreme Courts of Missouri and the Supreme Courts of Kansas and Montana have decisions [14] to the effect that, in case the state has failed to adopt textbooks, the local school officials may do so. This is due to the fact that the legislature has already given the power of general control over the schools into the hands of the local school corporation.

In 1908 the Missouri Appellate Court [15] ruled that, in case neither the state nor the local school board had made an adoption of textbooks, the teacher was the most logical agency for such adoption because of his familiarity with the relative merits of textbooks.

Does the Adoption of Uniform Textbooks Create an Illegal Monopoly?

Does the granting of exclusive privileges, through the adopting of particular textbooks and the contracting with individuals for the exclusive right to furnish such adopted textbooks, fall within the prohibition of the law against monopolies? The United States Circuit Court of the Oregon District in 1879 expressed an opinion [16] concerning the right of a state in this matter. In part the Court said:

> The legislature may exercise it (the police power) by contracting with any one to furnish books of a prescribed character and cost for the use of said schools for a definite period. To authorize and provide that, by means of contract, or legislative grant, a particular person or persons shall have the exclusive right to do or furnish a particular thing, upon certain conditions, for the use and convenience of the public, has always been a common mode of exercising the police powers of the state and unless the constitution imposes some limitation upon the power of the legislature on this subject its action is final and binding.

A number of cases [17] have been found in which the Court held in agreement with the position of the United States Court given above. The Nevada Supreme Court [17] in 1883 made use of the same language in deciding this issue. The Indiana Supreme Court [8] in discussing this issue in 1889 expressed its opinion in part as follows:

> The statute is not within the constitutional provisions directed against monopolies. It designates as the standard for the guidance of the State Board of Education certain books, requires that the books furnished for the use of the schools shall be equal in merit to those named . . . and requires the board to award the contract to the lowest bidder. . . . There is no exclusion of bidders, no limitation of the right to furnish school books to the people of the state to any class; on the contrary, all who are prepared to supply such books as the statute makes the standard are invited to compete for the contract. No special privilege is granted to any one, no right denied to any one, for all are invited to enter the field as competitors; . . . If the right of regulation and control exists, then the fact that the exercise of the right does exclude some publisher is an inseparable and unavoidable

condition of the exercise of that right. Without it the right is an-
nihilated.

The Procedure of Adoption

(1) *The Agencies of Adoption.* Concerning the agency for
the adoption of textbooks, the following statement [18], supported by a number of decisions, is found in Lawyers' Reports
Annotated:

The general rule seems to be that the authority to select textbooks
is generally vested in some public officer or board, and that the action
of the agency designated is conclusive, so that the pupil and his parent
or guardian has no voice in the matter.

The agency for adoption in many states [18] is the State
Board of Education. Some states have a State Textbook Commission [19] which may or may not be made up entirely or in
part from the members of the State Board of Education.

It was shown in Section (1) "Who Has the Power Over the
Adoption of Textbooks" that in some instances [9, 13, 14, 15]
the officials of the local school corporations might become the
agency for the selection of textbooks.

(2) *The Receipt of Bids for Furnishing Textbooks.* How
strictly should the provisions of a statute regulating the receipt
of bids for textbooks be followed? The Supreme Court [20]
of Utah took what seems to be a sensible position in a case in
1902. The statute required that there should be a convention of
state and county school officials called to select textbooks; and
that this convention should "publicly open and read proposals
by book companies to furnish textbooks." At this convention
proposals were received from some thirty-five or forty companies. Many companies had submitted voluminous catalogues
and samples as a part of their bids. The Court took the position that, in all essential things, strict compliance with a statute
that dealt with the opening of bids and the letting of contracts
for textbooks was necessary; that in such situations, where the
welfare of the pupils and the conservation of public funds were
concerned, it was important that the rights of all be safeguarded.
However, the Court held that the public opening of the bids and
the public reading of the introductory part of each bid were
sufficient; that they constituted substantial compliance with

the statutory requirement, and therefore were sufficient. The Court stated the rule governing its decision as follows:

It is a common rule (21) of statutory construction that, when language construed in a strict and liberal sense would lead to an absurdity, such language should be liberally construed, when by so doing the object and purpose of the statute will be accomplished.

(3) *Conditions Necessary to Adoption.* In construing a statute which required that the State Board of Education "prescribe and cause to be adopted" a uniform series of textbooks, the Nevada Supreme Court [22] in 1883 seems to have gone very far to uphold the action of the State Board in a matter of adoption of textbooks. The Board had met and passed a resolution selecting a certain company's textbook and authorizing the secretary to contract for the same. Two days later, before a contract had been signed, the Board voted to reconsider its action. It later prescribed and adopted another company's book. In deciding the case between the first company and the Board, the Court held that, although the Board had met and "prescribed" a certain textbook, it had not done anything towards "adopting" it into the schools; that the two things had to be done before the Board was bound to the publisher. Therefore, the Board was within its rights when it reconsidered its action of "prescription" and proceeded to "prescribe and cause to be adopted" the book of another company.

The Kansas Supreme Court [23] in 1892 decided an interesting case involving this matter. The statute required that the Textbook Board of the state should approve the bond of a publisher before the adoption of the textbook which he proposed to furnish should be complete. The Board in this case determined the amount of the bond but adjourned before the bond itself had been filed and approved. Later a committee of the Board approved the bond but in a smaller amount than had been determined by the Board. The Court decided that there had been no adoption in this case.

The Texas Supreme Court [24] in 1923 held that, where the statute made it the duty of the State Board of Education to adopt textbooks and the duty of the State Superintendent of Public Instruction to perform the ministerial duties connected with the purchase and distribution of such books, anything that the State Superintendent did in the way of adopting textbooks would not constitute a legal adoption; that he could not execute a contract for such textbooks that would be binding as against the state, or upon which the textbook publisher could maintain an action. The same Court [25] decided a case in 1924 in which the selection of the textbook had been made, the contract signed, and the amount of the bond determined, but the Board had adjourned before the publisher's bond had been signed by the Governor and returned to the Board. The Court held that this contract was neither void nor voidable.

The Arkansas Supreme Court [19] expressed its opinion concerning the conditions necessary to the adoption of textbooks in part as follows:

> Our conclusion is that under the statute authorizing this contract there can be no consummation until formal execution of the writing required by the statute and the approval of the bond which the statute also requires; nor could there be any presumed intention of the parties to consummate the contract prior to the fulfillment of these details.

Contracts to Furnish Adopted Textbooks

Contracts to furnish adopted textbooks are necessarily made with the state or some school corporation which is a part of the state government. A very important rule of law that has to do with contracts intended to bind the state was stated by the United States Circuit Court [16] of the Oregon District in 1879 as follows:

> But it is a well settled rule of law, that the state is not bound by the acts of its agents, unless it manifestly appears that they were acting within the scope of their authority; and individuals as well as courts must take notice of the nature and extent of the authority conferred by law upon a person acting in an official capacity.

On this same point the United States Supreme Court [26] in 1876 said in part:

> It is thought better that an individual should occasionally suffer from the mistakes of public officers or agents, than to adopt a rule which, through improper combination or collusion, might be turned to the detriment and injury of the public.

The attitude of the Kentucky Court of Appeals [27] in construing contracts for the furnishing of textbooks was expressed in a decision handed down in 1914. When called upon to construe the School Textbook Commission Law this Court said in part:

> The one demand for this legislation, the one purpose sought to be accomplished, the one interest of those favoring the Act, was to protect the consumer, to procure for the users of school textbooks the lowest prices for which such books could be sold anywhere. The object of the legislature was to benefit the last purchaser—the people. The law was enacted in the interest of this class, and this class alone.
>
> The legislature fully understood that the publishers and the retail dealers could take care of themselves without any assistance from the law-making power,—if it should be conceded that the lawmaking power could legally assist them; and that no provision of the act was intended to advance the interest of either.

The Tennessee Supreme Court [18] in 1899 expressed an attitude much similar to that expressed by the Kentucky Court.

In 1925 the Arkansas Supreme Court [19] laid down a rule to the effect that the agency of the state that performs the duty of selecting textbooks and contracting for them for a specified term may recede from negotiations concerning such adoption and contract for any reason, however capricious, at any time before the formal signing of a contract or before the performance of any act of discretion yet undone by the agency for the state. The Indiana Appellate Court [28] had made substantially the same ruling in 1904.

The Licensing or Registration of Textbooks

The Illinois Supreme Court [29] in 1911 decided that a statute which required publishers of textbooks to license all textbooks offered for sale in the State of Illinois was not rendered unconstitutional as a result of the action of the publishers in refusing so to license their books, even though their action made it impossible for school corporations to purchase legal books. The holding of the Court in part follows:

> The legislature cannot compel publishers to license their books if they choose not to offer them for sale in this state, but it does have the power, as a condition precedent to their right to sell them for use in the public schools of this state, to require them to license them.

In 1920 the Illinois Supreme Court [30] upheld a different statute which provided for a method of licensing or registering the publications of publishing companies with the State Superintendent of Public Instruction. According to this statute the book companies were required to file copies of the publications which they proposed to sell for use in the public schools in Illinois, also a proposition stating prices for the new books, exchange prices, etc. The statute also required the filing of an undertaking, accompanied by a bond, to furnish such books in accordance with the proposition on file for a period of five years from the date of filing. Prices went up rapidly after 1917. The statute provided that, upon the filing of a new undertaking by a book company, the State Superintendent should transmit the new price list to all the school corporations in Illinois. A book company furnished the State Superintendent with a new price list for their books. The prices were higher. The company entered suit to mandate the Superintendent to transmit this price list to all the school corporations in Illinois. The Court held that the Superintendent should not transmit this price list; that the undertaking first filed held good for the full five years, notwithstanding the unexpected and unusual increase in prices. The United States Circuit Court of Appeals [31] in 1921 upheld this Illinois statute. The Court held that this statute, together with the acts of the publisher in filing a list of textbooks, an undertaking to furnish such books for a term of five years, and a bond guaranteeing performance, constituted a contract to furnish such books to any school corporation that should adopt such books at any time during the term of five years from the filing date. A Michigan statute of this same general nature was upheld by the United States District Court [32] in 1920.

Compulsory Use of State-Adopted Textbooks

The attitude assumed by the courts of a number of states [10 and 11] toward the power of the state to compel the use of state-adopted textbooks is indicated by the following quotation from [8] the Indiana Supreme Court:

We can find neither reason nor authority that suggests a doubt as to the power of the legislature to require a designated series of books to be used in the schools and to require that the books selected shall be obtained from the person to whom the contract for supplying them may be awarded.

The Missouri Supreme Court [33] in 1892 decided that a statute which forbade the use of any textbook other than the state-adopted books did not violate the constitution because it was not an invasion of the duties of "supervision of instruction" vested by the constitution in the State Board of Education.

What may the publisher do in case his book, regularly adopted, is not used? The Washington Supreme Court [34] in 1904 held that, unless the publisher has been materially damaged by the failure of the offending school corporation to use the adopted textbook, he is not entitled to relief by injunction.

The United States Supreme Court [35] has stated the rule followed by that court in construing grants of franchises and special privileges, as follows:

> Grants of franchises and special privileges are always to be construed most strongly against the donee and in favor of the public.

The United States Courts have followed this rule [36] in a number of decisions.

Sufficiency of Use of State-Adopted Textbooks

The question of sufficiency of use of an adopted textbook is one which may affect the curriculum of the public schools. The Washington Supreme Court [34] had four cases before it in 1904 that involved this issue. In each of them the local school corporation had failed to use the adopted textbook to the satisfaction of the publisher. The Court decided that a local school board had no right to establish a course of study which was inconsistent with the state course of study; that it had no right to use supplementary books or to fail to use the adopted books so that as a result the sales of a company holding the exclusive right to furnish the adopted textbook would be reduced.

CHANGE OF TEXTBOOKS

The attitude of the courts toward the change of textbooks is clearly shown by the following cases. The California Supreme Court [37] in 1875 held that after a textbook had been regularly adopted the statute had to be strictly followed as to its use and as to its change. This Court declared that, where a notice was required to terminate an indefinite period of use, such notice must conform strictly to the statute. The United

States Circuit Court [38] in 1889 took the position that the laws concerning the adoption, use, and change of textbooks should be strictly followed because they were intended to assure and protect the rights of the people.

This attitude of favoring the people is made more emphatic in a case decided by the Kentucky Court of Appeals [39] in 1909. The statute provided that, after a school board had adopted a textbook, it might not change the book except after a year's notice and upon the affirmative votes of not less than two-thirds of the members. In this case textbooks had been adopted but no contract made with the publisher. An attempt was made to change the textbooks without strict compliance with the statute. A company whose books were to be discarded asked for an injunction. In denying the injunction the Court said in part:

> The legislation which requires the establishment by public authority of a uniform system of education by adopting and maintaining, till deliberately changed by adequate public authority, such textbooks as may have been selected in the public schools of the city, is a measure solely for the benefit of the public—the patrons of the schools.
> The publishers are not the subject at all of the legislative action. It was never intended by it to confer any right upon them, or to allow them to interfere in the matter in any way.

A similar attitude is indicated in the decision of the New York Superintendent [40] in 1887 in upholding the action of a local school board. This board had made an adoption of a textbook. Before any of the parties interested had acted upon the adoption, the board changed the adoption to another book. There was some question as to whether the board had followed its own by-laws strictly in the reconsideration of the first adoption. However, the Superintendent held that the latter adoption should be allowed to stand as against the publisher of the book first adopted. This same desire to protect the public against excessive changing of textbooks is evident in the decisions [41] of the Supreme Court of South Carolina and the Kentucky Court of Appeals in interpreting a statutory requirement that not more than 50 per cent of the textbooks subject to change shall be changed by the board in charge of adoption.

THE TREND OF THE DECISIONS

There is a noticeable trend in the decisions toward a stricter interpretation and construction of statutes in favor of the public or those who buy textbooks as against those who are seeking or who may be granted special privileges in the nature of exclusive adoptions of and contracts for the furnishing of textbooks.

The decisions show a continuing trend of liberality of interpretation and construction of issues in favor of advancing the cause of education and the public schools.

These trends are not shown by lines of cases occurring in any one jurisdiction, but by the cases as a whole which deal with the issues of the adoption and change of textbooks.

CONCLUSIONS

1. A uniform system of common schools does not necessarily require a uniform series of textbooks.

2. As an indication of the liberality of the courts in construing the statutes favorably toward education the term "textbook" has been construed by one court as a general term in order to uphold a statute.

3. The term "uniform textbook" as used in Uniform Textbook Laws does not require that books by the same author in the same subject shall be used in all grades.

4. A "uniform series" of textbooks is construed to mean the whole series adopted for use in the schools and not as a set of books on one subject necessarily by the same author.

5. The power of adoption and control of textbooks for the public schools is vested solely and exclusively in the legislature, unless specifically restricted and controlled by the state constitution.

6. It is a quite general rule that in the absence of an adoption by the state or of specific legislative provision for the same, the local school officials (board or trustee) may adopt textbooks.

7. The adoption of particular textbooks and the contracting with persons for the exclusive right to furnish adopted books for a term of years, as commonly practiced, does not fall within the prohibition of the law against monopolies.

8. The agencies of adoption of textbooks are agencies of the

state. Neither the parent nor the child has any power in the adoption.

9. Statutory provisions for the adoption, use, and change of textbooks will be strictly construed and enforced by the courts in favor of the public. These laws are enacted for the protection of the public.

10. He who deals with school officials is bound to take notice of the nature and extent of the authority conferred by the law upon the official.

11. The licensing and registration of textbooks and the filing of proposals with the state board to furnish such books has the force of a contract of which any or all school corporations in the state may take the benefit.

12. Mandamus will lie against school officials to compel the use of adopted texts and injunction will issue to restrain school officials from actions that materially decrease the sales of adopted textbooks.

CITATIONS ON CHAPTER VII

1. Offholder v. State, 51 Neb. 91.
2. People ex rel. Mack v. Board of Education Aurora, 175 Ill. 9.
3. Finegan, Decisions New York Supt., 1232.
4. Attorney General v. Detroit Board Education, 133 Mich. 689.
5. State v. Textbook Commission, 87 Kan. 781.
6. Curryer v. Merrill, 25 Minn. 1;
   Clarke v. Haworth, 122 Ind. 462;
   State v. Womack, 4 Wash. 19;
   Effingham v. Hamilton, 68 Mich. 523;
   Reno County School District v. Shadduck, 25 Kan. 467;
   Topeka Board Education v. Welch, 51 Kan. 792;
   Powell v. Board Education, 97 Ill. 375;
   Richards v. Raymond, 92 Ill. 612.
7. Campana v. Calderhead, 17 Mont. 548.
8. State v. Haworth, 122 Ind. 462.
9. People v. Board Education of Oakland, 55 Cal. 331.
10. State v. School Directors, 74 Mo. 21;
    State v. Board, 35 Ohio St. 368;
    School Commissioners v. State Board, 26 Md. 505;
    Robinson v. Howard, 84 N. C. 151;
    Stuart v. School District No. 1, 30 Mich. 69;
    Ford v. Kendall Borough School District, 121 Pa. St. 543;
    People v. Board, 101 Ill. 308;
    Richards v. Raymond, 92 Ill. 612;
    Powell v. Board, 97 Ill. 375;
    Briggs v. Johnson County, 4 Dill. 148;

Rawson v. Spencer, 113 Mass. 40;
Commonwealth v. Hartman, 17 Pa. St. 118;
Leeper v. State, 103 Tenn. 500.

11. State v. Haworth, 122 Ind. 462;
Hovey v. State, 119 Ind. 395;
Hovey v. State ex rel. Riley, 119 Ind. 386;
State v. Harmon, 31 Ohio St. 250;
State v. Hawkins, 44 Ohio St. 98;
Silver Burdett & Co. v. Indiana State Board of Education, 35 Ind. App. 438;
Leeper v. State, 103 Tenn. 500.

12. Schroder v. City of St. Paul, 115 Minn. 222.

13. State v. Webber, 108 Ind. 31;
State v. School District, 31 Neb. 552;
Knabe v. Board of Education, 67 Mich. 262.

14. State v. Millsap, 131 Mo. App. 683;
Derkins v. Gore, 85 Mo. 485;
Campana v. Calderhead, 17 Mont. 548;
State v. Hamilton, 42 Mo. App. 24;
Epley v. Hall, 97 Kan. 549.

15. State v. Millsap, 131 Mo. App. 683.

16. Bancroft v. Thayer, 2 Federal cases, Case 835.

17. State v. State Board Education, 18 Nev. 173;
People v. Board Education, 55 Cal. 331;
People v. State Board Education, 44 Cal. 684;
State v. Blue, 122 Ind. 600;
Leeper v. State, 103 Tenn. 500.

18. 36 Lawyers' Report Annotated 277;
School Commissioners v. State Board Education, 26 Md. 505;
State v. Bronson, 115 Mo. 271;
State v. Haworth, 122 Ind. 462;
Hovey v. State, 119 Ind. 386 and 395;
State v. Hawkins, 44 Ohio St. 98;
State v. Harmon, 31 Ohio St. 250;
Leeper v. State, 103 Tenn. 500.

19. McRae v. Farquhar & Albright, 269 S. W. (Ark.) 375;
Owens v. Heywood, 58 S. E. (S. C.) 1095;
State v. Shawkey, 93 S. E. (W. Va.) 759.

20. Tanner v. Nelson, 25 Utah 226.

21. Van Fleet v. Van Fleet, 49 Mich. 610;
Smith v. People, 47 N. Y. 330;
People v. Davenport, 91 N. Y. 574;
Mayor v. Root, 8 Md. 95;
Swift & Givins' Appeal, 111 Pa. St. 516;
Lau Ow Bew v. United States, 144 U. S. 47.

22. State v. State Board of Education, 18 Nev. 173.

23. Maynard v. Olsen, 48 Kan. 565.

24. American Book Co. v. Marrs, 253 S. W. (Tex.) 817.

25. Scribners' Sons v. Marrs, 262 S. W. (Tex.) 722.
26. Whiteside v. U. S., 93 U. S. 257.
27. Bowman v. Hamlett, 159 Ky. 184.
28. Silver Burdett & Co. v. Indiana State Board, 35 Ind. App. 438.
29. Palzin v. Rand, McNally Co., 250 Ill. 561.
30. People ex rel. Albright v. Blair, 292 Ill. 139.
31. Scribner's Sons v. Board, 278 Fed. 366.
32. Macmillan Co. v. Johnson, 269 Fed. 28.
33. State v. Bronson, 115 Mo. 271.
34. Westland Publishing Co. v. Royal, 36 Wash. 399;
    Rand, McNally & Co. v. Royal, 36 Wash. 420;
    Wagner v. Royal, 36 Wash. 428;
    Eaton v. Royal, 36 Wash. 435.
35. Turnpike Co. v. Illinois, 96 U. S. 63.
36. Slidell v. Grandjean, 111 U. S. 412;
    Navigation Co. v. Railway Co., 130 U. S. 1;
    Ivinson v. Board of School Commissioners, 39 Fed. Rep. 735.
37. Billmer v. State, 49 Cal. 684.
38. Ivinson v. Board School Commissioners, 39 Fed. Rep. 735.
39. Allyn & Bacon v. Louisville School Board, 131 Ky. 324.
40. Finegan, Judicial Decisions New York Supt., 1231.
41. State ex rel. Addy v. State Board Education, 94 S. E. (S. C.) 110;
    State Textbook Commissioner v. Weathers, 184 Ky. 748.

CHAPTER VIII

GENERAL SUMMARY OF FINDINGS

No attempt has been made to collect all the findings of this study under classified heads in this chapter. The findings are not cumulative in a way that admit of such treatment. They are so varied that there would be little significance in such a summary, granted that it could be made. The reader must turn to the chapter summaries for detailed information brought out by the study. An attempt has been made to present some statements that summarize the most important findings as set forth in the chapter summaries.

THE TREND OF THE DECISIONS

1. There has been a general trend of the decisions toward the more complete recognition of the power and duty of the state legislature and the local school corporations to provide a more extended public school organization and a more varied offering of particular secular subject matter in the public schools.

2. There has been a trend of the decisions toward the exclusion of all religious instruction as such, or religious influence whatsoever, from the public schools.

3. The trend of the decisions has been toward the recognition of the inherent right of the child to an education and a consequent trend toward the decrease of the parent's absolute control over his child's opportunity for an education.

4. The trend of the decisions has been toward favoring the public as against those persons who have been given special privileges in regard to furnishing instructional supplies to school corporations and to the public.

5. There has been a trend of the decisions toward upholding the power of the local school corporation to provide, upon its own initiative, instructional equipment for its schools.

6. There has lately been a suggestion of a trend toward greater participation of the federal courts in the adjudication of controversies involving the curriculum.

CONCERNING THE COURTS

The courts have no power to make prescriptions concerning the curriculum. They can only adjudicate particular cases that may be brought before them. The outcome of a case may vitally affect the curriculum. The courts have construed the statutes relating to the adoption, use, and change of textbooks, strictly, in favor of the public, as against the person holding or seeking to obtain special privileges relating to the furnishing of textbooks. They will not interfere with the discretion of school officials unless it appears that their action has been unconstitutional or illegal, or unless such action has amounted to an abuse of the power vested in the official. They have no power to institute any action on their own motion.

THE LEGISLATURE'S CONTROL OF THE CURRICULUM

1. The only limitation upon the power of the legislature to control the curriculum and, in fact, to establish, maintain, and control the entire public school system is the constitution.

2. The legislature may delegate to officials, boards, or local school corporations whatever part of its power over the curriculum and the public schools it may see fit to bestow upon them. It may also remove this power at its own pleasure.

3. The decisions uphold the power of the legislature to prescribe particular secular subject matter for the curriculum, to exclude subject matter from the curriculum, and to add organized curricular units to the curriculum of the public schools, subject only to restrictions that may be in the constitution.

4. Although the power of the legislature to make certain prescriptions concerning the curriculum of schools other than public schools has not been denied, nevertheless, the United States Supreme Court has decided that the legislature has not the power to exclude the teaching of foreign languages from the curriculum of such schools.

5. The legislature may require the officials and the school corporations, which it has created, to carry out any measures which it may see fit to adopt.

6. Any person dealing with public school officials is bound by the statutory limitations of their power and he must satisfy himself as to what those limitations are.

7. The power to control the adoption, use, and change of

textbooks is vested solely and exclusively in the legislature, but it may be delegated to such agencies or local school corporations as the legislature in its discretion considers to be for the best interests of the schools and the public.

THE LOCAL SCHOOL CORPORATION'S CONTROL
OF THE CURRICULUM

1. The powers of the local school corporation over the curriculum and its schools in general are only such as are vested in it by the legislature. It has no inherent powers.

2. The decisions uphold the power of the local school corporation to add to or to classify the curriculum of its local schools at its discretion, subject, however, to constitutional and statutory limitations.

3. Officials of the local school corporations may make all reasonable rules and regulations necessary to the control of their curriculum and their schools, subject only to constitutional and statutory provisions.

4. The decisions seem to uphold the power of the local school corporation's officials to exercise their discretion in the provision of whatever general instructional equipment they may deem necessary for the best interests of the schools.

5. The higher courts seem not to have been asked to pass upon the power of local school corporations to furnish individual instructional equipment, other than textbooks.

6. The higher courts have universally held that specific statutory authority is necessary to enable a local school corporation to provide free textbooks.

7. The courts have disapproved of school officials assuming any relations whereby they might profit financially by the sale of instructional equipment.

CONTROL OF THE CURRICULUM BY PARENT AND PUPIL

1. Courts and legislatures now recognize that the child has a legal right to an education, which it is the function and duty of the state legislature to provide, and which the parent must enable his child to secure.

2. The parent's former absolute control over the education of his child has been reduced by legislative enactment and judicial interpretation.

3. The parent, according to the weight of the decisions, seems still to have a right, as against the local school corporation's prescription of studies, to make a reasonable selection from the studies offered.

4. The parent has an inherent constitutional right to have his child instructed in any school which meets the minimum standards that the legislature, acting within its constitutional powers, may have prescribed.

5. Neither the parent nor the pupil has any control over the adoption of textbooks.

THE ELEMENTS OF A PUBLIC SCHOOL AND A UNIFORM SYSTEM OF SCHOOLS

1. The decisions have isolated the following essential elements of a public or common school. It must be free, open equally to all, and under complete public control.

2. The elements of a uniform system of public schools which were isolated in the cases studied are (a) that there must be uniformity in executive administration and in the power given to similar officials; (b) that there is no need for limitations upon the studies presented; (c) that uniform textbooks throughout the state are unnecessary.

RELIGION AND THE BIBLE IN THE PUBLIC SCHOOLS

A summary of the decisions on "Religion and the Bible in the Public Schools" that is more general than that made at the close of Chapter V is very difficult to make without mere repetition of the points as given there. There are too few common elements in the cases that have been decided to allow of more generalization than has been made except as to a few points. These will be given here, but it will be necessary for the reader to make use of the detailed analysis of the cases from the different states, the facts assembled in Table I, and the additional summary in that chapter in order to understand the position of the courts in the various states. It is unnecessary to repeat those details here.

The decisions show that the matter of religion and the Bible in the public schools has been a source of controversies which have been carried before the higher judicial tribunals for adjudication since 1837. Up until the time of the final collection of the data for this study in 1926 this matter had been before the courts of 19 states in one form or another. It has been contended in each case that the practice complained of violated the constitutional guarantee of individual rights. Generally speaking, the constitutional provisions of the states from which these decisions come, the statutory enactments, and the decisions of the courts have attempted to avoid controversies and the infringement of individual rights by prohibiting offensive manifestations of religious attitudes, impulses, and associations in connection with the public schools.

The sources of controversy include such things as Bible reading, prayer, hymn singing, the wearing of distinctive religious garb, the use of sectarian buildings as places in which to hold public schools, the giving of school credit for outside Bible study, the placing of the Bible in a public school library, holding public school commencements in churches with prayer as a part of the program, requiring pupils to maintain a particular attitude during prayer in a public school, and excusing pupils from public school at the request of parents in order that the children might attend outside religious instruction.

The claims of unconstitutionality or illegality of the practices objected to have been based upon the following: (1) that such practices result in the appropriation and use of public funds in aid of sectarian purposes, (2) that the practices violate the right of freedom of conscience and liberty of worship of such pupils as object to them, (3) that the practices constitute forbidden religious and sectarian instruction or influence, (4) that the practice of excusing children to attend religious instruction violates the compulsory attendance laws.

The complainants in the cases studied have included Protestants, Catholics, Jews, and non-believers in the Bible.

The purposes of conducting those exercises that have religious significance have included the following: (1) the Bible was used purely as a textbook, (2) the exercises were admitted to be for the purpose of religious instruction, (3) the exercises were for the purpose of moral training.

The courts seem to agree only upon the following: (1) that sectarian instruction in the public schools is prohibited, (2) that the public schools should not be subjected to sectarian influence,

(3) that the public funds should not be appropriated or used in aid of sectarian purposes, (4) that no one should be compelled to attend or to support any worship against his will. However, when it comes to determining when the practices complained of constitute a violation of these propositions, there seems to be no general agreement.

There is a wide variation in the constitutional and statutory provisions of the different states, as well as the facts under which the decisions in the different states have been given.

CHAPTER IX

CONCLUSION

The conclusions that can be drawn from the findings of this study are not such as can be stated with certainty and exactness. Controversies that are carried to the higher courts of our country usually have elements of law and reason on either side of the issues presented. It is not possible to determine beforehand how a court will decide a case, even with the advice of the most able counsel, with all the facts of the case at hand, and with the law of the particular jurisdiction available. However, that was not the purpose of this study. As stated in the introduction, it has not been the purpose of this study to attempt to advise the reader what the law in any jurisdiction is to-day nor what the legal rights of an individual might be in any legal controversy over the curriculum. The reader must use this study as a source of information concerning the position of certain courts upon particular issues that have been decided by them and as an aid to his own thinking relative to similar curricular problems in which he may be interested. However, the findings do warrant the drawing of certain general conclusions as to the probable future attitude of the courts upon issues, the decision of which will probably have an important bearing upon the future of the curriculum of the public schools.

It is believed by the author that nowhere else in this country can evidences of more careful, considerate, and conscientious thinking upon curricular problems be found than in the opinions of the judges of the courts of the land. After a year of intensive study of the decisions relating to the curriculum of the public schools the author has a feeling of great confidence in the courts in regard to the adjudication of curricular controversies. This feeling is not founded upon the extent to which the courts agree with one another, for they do not so agree. Nor is it founded upon the author's agreement with the weight of the decisions upon the issues or upon any one of them. It is founded rather upon the evidences in the decisions themselves which show

156

apparently honest, sincere, and painstaking effort on the part of the judges to decide the cases according to sound principles of law and the facts presented.

There is an abundance of evidence in the decisions to the effect that the courts have had the best interests of the public schools of the United States at heart; that they have sought to further the development of an adequate, efficient, and well-administered system of public schools; that they have sought to protect the interests of all parties concerned; that they have attempted to lessen the causes of curricular controversies in all their decisions. There are fewer evidences of susceptibility on the part of the courts to hasty judgment, bias, prejudice, or undue influence of any sort, even in times of great public stress, strain, and emotion, than on the part of any other class of persons whose actions have been involved in the cases studied, whether it be the legislature, school officials, teachers, parents, pupils, the public, or even the religious organizations.

The trend of the decisions of the courts gives good grounds for concluding that the several courts will continue the tendencies shown in the past; that they will continue to favor the extension of a public school curriculum of secular subjects and curriculum units which will meet the needs of the child as a progressive civilization reveals them; that they will continue to guard the curriculum against the inclusion of practices that may have a tendency to disorganize and injure the schools; that they will continue to recognize the right of the child to an education; that they will continue to safeguard the public in regard to the expense incident to the public school system, while favoring proper instructional equipment and opportunities for the pupils; that they will continue to hold that a public or common school must be free, open equally to all and under complete public control.

There are good reasons for concluding that the legislatures of the various states will continue to control the curriculum of the public schools much the same as in the past. The federal and state constitutions provide the only limitations upon the legislature's complete and exclusive control of the entire public school system, the curriculum included of course. A court of competent jurisdiction can only interfere with this power when a particular case has been brought before it as a result of the legislature's violation of the constitutional provisions. The state courts are, judging from the decisions, less likely to interfere than are the federal courts, but one can confidently predict that such constitutional violations will be effectually prevented by the courts.

It is reasonable to expect that the detailed control of the curriculum of the public schools by the state will continue to increase. The inequalities of the curricular offerings of local school corporations, the increasing recognition of the state's obligation to equalize educational opportunity, and the burden of taxation will force such a result. It is to be expected that an increase in legislative prescriptions in regard to the curriculum will occur in response to the demands of popular sentiment or at the insistence of well organized and powerful groups of citizens. Such attempts are being made in all the states. It should be the purpose of the teaching profession to carry on curriculum studies and research constantly. This profession should make the facts that are necessary for intelligent action available to all citizens for their consideration. It should coöperate and work with all agencies that seek truly to improve the subject matter of instruction through legislative action or through particular prescriptions to the end that whatever legislative action may be taken and whatever prescriptions may be made as to the curriculum shall be responsive to the needs of the children that are to be educated, and shall not be restrictive of the public school's efforts to serve all the children of the state in their search for truth.

The number of curricular activities in which the local school officials participate may be expected to increase. A part of this increase may come from local initiative but much of it may be expected to come about as a result of the continued increase in the prescriptions concerning the curriculum resulting from legislative action. As the detailed control of the curriculum by the state increases it means (1) that the comparative amount of control left to either the local school corporation or the parent must necessarily decrease, (2) that more of the detail of the local school corporation's control over its own curriculum will be regulated through state administrative and supervisory officials whose offices and duties have been established by the legislature. The local school corporations are creatures of the state and have only such powers as are given to them by statute or constitution.

As the state through its various agencies assumes greater and greater detailed control over the curriculum, the relative responsibility of the state and its personal representatives for the effect produced by the curriculum upon the child becomes correspondingly greater. This aspect of the situation should not be neglected. It is not unreasonable to conclude that some portion of the much discussed and supposed decrease in the disciplinary power of the modern home is the result of removing from the parent a considerable portion of his responsibility for the education of his child. There is every reason to conclude that the courts will continue to uphold the power of the local school officials to make all reasonable rules and regulations for the necessary carrying out of the duties and obligations placed upon them by the statutes in connection with the establishment, maintenance, and control of a local system of schools and a curriculum for them.

The evidence of the decisions seems to warrant the conclusion that the rights of the child to an education will continue to be recognized and that the courts will favor any increase in the rights of the child that may seem best for the child and for the state. While the decisions make it clear that the common-law rights of the parent to control the education of his child will not be allowed to work injury to the child, yet the decisions seem to warrant the conclusion that the courts will continue to uphold the reasonable rights of the parent as against the curricular prescriptions of the local school officials. There is good reason for concluding that the federal courts may come to exercise a considerable influence in determining curricular controversies. There seems to be a tendency to attempt to carry such controversies to the federal courts, particularly in cases where the rights of parents and children are concerned. The decisions made in the federal courts in the so-called language cases and in the Oregon compulsory public school attendance amendment seem to warrant a conclusion that perhaps the federal courts will construe such acts of the legislature, or even of the people, rather strictly in favor of the parent and the child.

There are very good reasons for concluding that the higher courts of the various states will continue in the main to view the matter of religion and the Bible in their public schools in much the same light in which it has been viewed in the decisions

already made in their state. Such courts are prone to continue
a position that has once been assumed in their jurisdiction, particularly in regard to such a controversial matter. However,
there are also good reasons for believing that the trend of the
decisions over the entire country will continue to be toward the
exclusion of manifestations of the religious impulse from the
public schools, not because the judges are opposed to religion,
for the decisions show that they are not, but because such manifestations are provocative of controversy, ill will, and injury to
the public schools and to society.

In the decisions studied, even in those in which various manifestations of the religious impulse have been forbidden, the judges
have plainly indicated their faith in the efficacy of religion as
a means of moral stimulation and growth for the individual and
for society. However, the judges show that they realize the
harm that can come to the schools and to the state from dissen-
sion and controversies and evidently have had that in mind at
all times when deliberating upon the rights of the parties involved in the cases brought before them. They realize that
public funds and property must not be appropriated or used
in aid of sectarian organizations or influences, but they find it
difficult to decide whether the facts of a particular case bring
the action complained of within the prohibition of the law.
They recognize that an individual has an inherent constitutional
right to freedom of conscience and liberty of worship, but the
borderline of the actions complained of is being pushed to such
extreme limits that the difficulty of deciding when infringement
of these individual rights occurs, increases constantly. They
agree that sectarian instruction is entirely out of place and prohibited in the public schools, but the acts complained of tend to
become more and more inconsequential as time passes and this
brings greater difficulty in drawing distinctions between those
acts that are prohibited and those that do not amount to a violation under the particular provisions of the constitution or the
statute. The courts are also agreed that the public schools should
not be subjected to sectarian influence, but just when such influence has occurred to a degree that falls within the prohibition
of the law is a question of great difficulty.

There seem to be reasonable grounds for asserting that many
of the particular causes for complaint relative to religion and

the Bible in the public schools may not have occurred to the minds of those who drafted our constitutional provisions regarding the relation of religion and the state. Whether they fall within the principles set forth in the constitutions or the statutes is the question that the courts are forced to answer. The issues of a case before a court are necessarily affirmed by one side and denied by the other. The court is forced to decide one way or the other upon the issues presented. Herein lies the difficulty. It does seem to be going very far indeed to insist that the freedom of conscience and the liberty of worship of the individual is violated by the general invocation of a minister or a priest when delivered at the commencement exercises of a public school that are being held in a church, or to insist that the placing of a copy of the Bible in a public school library for reference purposes is prohibited. What course should our courts pursue? Should they take the position that any act, however inconsequential, of any one connected with the public schools and which is suggestive of religious connections or manifestations should be construed to be a violation of the law, even though there be but a single individual complaining? Shall every bit of subject matter that is suggestive of religion and to which a single individual objects be removed from the curriculum of the public schools?

Such a curriculum would be absurd. Mathematics and a little science would be about all that would be left. Even the literature of a dead language could not meet such a test. Evidently there must be some place at which such a procedure must stop before it produces absurdity. Society must provide some means of deciding such issues. The author is convinced that the courts of our land constitute the best means yet devised by society to perform this function. However, it does not solve the problem to rely solely upon the courts to solve such controversial problems. Their agencies are the decision of individual cases, the issuing of writs of mandamus, and the granting of injunctions against certain practices. Mandamus and injunction are extraordinary remedies. Injunctions are particularly restrictive. Society should not have to depend upon such measures to compel the observation of the law or respect for the rights of others. The highest type of religious ideal or even that of a purely moral ideal, granted that such an ideal be possible, surely does not contemplate a state of society governed by mandate or injunction of the courts.

As long as there are Protestant school authorities who prescribe that the King James Bible shall be read in their schools it may be expected that there will be Catholics, Jews, or non-believers in the Bible who will object to the practice and cause controversies. As long as there are Catholic school officials of the public schools who attempt to conduct public schools in parochial school buildings with Sisters in distinctive garb as teachers there will be Protestants, Jews, or non-believers who will object and institute lawsuits. Whenever those who wish to destroy the influence of the Bible seek opportunity to prevent the least bit of assistance by public school officials to an outside program of religious instruction, they arouse bitter animosities and feelings on the part of those who favor such a program.

Just as long as any one group of persons seeks its own advantage or attempts to coerce other groups or individuals, opposition and bitter resentment may be expected. Just as long as some men are more concerned with the form of their worship, with creeds and dogma, than they are with the spirit in which they pay reverence to the Supreme Being, manifestations of the religious impulse in the public schools will continue to arouse turmoil, strife, hatred, and legal controversies, thus defeating what should be the aim of such exercises. So long as some people continue to hold to certain fixed and unalterable opinions concerning the Bible, while others take a more liberal view of it, the use of the Bible in the public schools will continue to provoke such controversies as it has in the past. So long as so-called religion and the Bible cause people to show the bitterness, the hatred, the intolerance, and the tendency to institute lawsuits that have been shown in the past, the courts may be expected to continue the trend toward the exclusion of religious manifestations from the curriculum of the public schools. The real solution of this difficulty concerning the curriculum of the public schools lies in the hope of a change in the hearts and attitudes of men. Whenever men come to be charitable enough of the opinions, the aspirations, and the hopes of their fellow men to respect their rights and their honest beliefs, then such difficulties as have arisen over religion and the Bible in the public schools will not have to be settled by the judgment, mandate, and injunction of the courts. Until that time approaches, the courts must be depended upon to pronounce final judgment upon our curricular controversies. It is the belief of the author that they are less susceptible to prejudice and undue influence than any of the other agencies that help to control the curriculum of the public schools to-day.

BIBLIOGRAPHY

American Decisions. Bancroft-Whitney Co. San Francisco, Cal.

American Digest. Century Edition, 1658-1896. Vol. XLIII, 1903; Decennial Edition, 1897-1906. Vol. XVII, 1910; Second Decennial Edition, 1907-1916; Vol. XX, 1923. Key Number Series, 1917-1925. Vols. IA-XX, 1917-1925. West Publishing Co., St. Paul, Minn.

American Law Register. University of Pennsylvania Press, Philadelphia, Pa.

American Law Reports, Annotated. Lawyers' Coöperative Publishing Co., Rochester, N. Y.

American Law Reports, Annotated. Edward Thompson Co., Northport, N. Y.

American Law Reports Annotated. Bancroft-Whitney Co., San Francisco, Cal.

American Law Reports. Bancroft-Whitney Co., San Francisco, Cal.

American State Reports. Bancroft-Whitney Co., San Francisco, Cal.

Annotated Cases, American and English. Edward Thompson Co., Northport, N. Y.

Annotated Cases, American and English. Bancroft-Whitney Co., San Francisco, Cal.

ATHEARN, WALTER S. *Indiana Survey of Religious Education in 1923-1924.* 3 Volumes. George H. Doran Co., New York City, N. Y.

Barnes' Federal Code. Edited by Uriah Barnes. Bobbs-Merrill Co., Indianapolis, Ind. 1919. pp. 2831.

Barnes' Federal Code 1923 Supplement. Edited by Uriah Barnes. Bobbs-Merrill Co., Indianapolis, Ind. 1923. pp. 1119.

BOYKIN, J. C., and HOOD, WILLIAM R. *Legislation and Judicial Decisions Relating to Education.* United States Bureau of Education Bulletin, 1913, Whole No. 566, No. 55.

BROWN, SAMUEL W. *Secularization of American Education Shown by State Constitutions and Court Decisions.* Ohio State University, Columbus, O. 1912. pp. 160.

BUTTERFIELD, ERNEST W. "The Relation of Religious Education to Public Instruction." *National Education Association, Department of Superintendence Official Report.* Washington, D. C. 1926. pp. 199-205.

CASE, ADELAIDE T. *Liberal Christianity and Religious Education.* Macmillan Co., New York City, N. Y. 1924. pp. 194.

COOLEY, ROGER W. *Brief Making and the Use of Law Books.* West Publishing Co., St. Paul, Minn. 1924. Vol I, pp. 1700; Vol. II, pp. 1040.

COOLEY, THOMAS M. *Treatise on the Constitutional Limitations Which Rest upon the Legislative Powers of States.* Little, Brown, and Co., Boston, Mass. 1903. pp. 1036.

Cyclopedia of Law and Procedure. Vol. XXXV. American Law Book Co., New York City, N. Y.

Essential Place of Religion in Education. Monograph published by National Education Association. 1916. Copies from D. W. Springer, Secretary, N.E.A. Ann Arbor, Mich.

Facts on the Public School Curriculum. National Education Association Research Bulletin, Vol. I, No. 5. Washington, D. C. 1924. pp. 31.

FLANDERS, JESSE K. *Legislative Control of the Elementary Curriculum.* Bureau of Publications, Teachers College, Columbia University, New York. 1925. pp. 242.

FINEGAN, THOMAS E. *Judicial Decisions of the State Superintendent of Common Schools, State Superintendent of Public Instruction, State Commissioner of Education from 1822 to 1913.* In Volume 2, Annual Report of the University of the State of New York, Albany, N. Y. 1914. pp. 1508.

HALL, ARTHUR J. *Religious Education in the Public Schools of the State and City of New York.* University of Chicago Press, Chicago, Ill. 1914. pp. 111.

HICKS, FREDERICK C. *Materials and Methods of Legal Research.* Lawyers' Coöperative Publishing Co., Rochester, N. Y. 1923. pp. 626.

HITES, LAIRD T. "Recent Legislation on Religion and the Public Schools." *Religious Education,* Vol. XX, No. 4. Aug., 1925. pp. 292-297.

HOOD, WILLIAM R. *Bible in the Public Schools.* United States Bureau of Education Bulletin, 1923, No. 15. pp. 13.

HOOD, WILLIAM R. *Digest of State Laws Relating to Public Education in Force January 1, 1915.* United States Bureau of Education Bulletin, 1915, No. 47.

HOOD, WILLIAM R. *Review of Educational Legislation, 1917 and 1918.* United States Bureau of Education Bulletin, 1919, No. 13.

HOOD, WILLIAM R. *Review of Educational Legislation, 1919 and 1920.* United States Bureau of Education Bulletin, 1922, No. 13.

HOOD, WILLIAM R. *Some Important School Legislation, 1921 and 1922.* United States Bureau of Education Bulletin, 1922, No. 43.

HOOD, WILLIAM R. *State Laws Relating to Education Enacted 1915, 1916, and 1917.* United States Bureau of Education Bulletin, 1918, No. 23.

HOOD, WILLIAM R. *State Laws Relating to Education Enacted 1918 and 1919.* United States Bureau of Education Bulletin 1920, No. 30.

HOOD, WILLIAM R. *State Laws Relating to Education Enacted 1920 and 1921.* United States Bureau of Education Bulletin, 1922. No. 20.

Index Digest of State Constitutions. Prepared for the New York State Constitutional Convention Commission by the Legislative Drafting Research Fund of Columbia University. J. B. Lyon Co., Albany, N. Y. 1915. pp. 1546.

Index to Legal Periodical Literature. Edited by Elsie Basset. Vol. 14-18, 1921-1925. Published in connection with the Law Library Journal. H. W. Wilson Co., New York City, N. Y.

Index to Legal Periodical Literature. Edited by Frank E. Chipman. Boston Book Co., Boston, Mass., Vol. III, 1898-1908, 1919; Vol. IV, 1908-1922, 1922.

Index to Legal Literature. Edited by Leonard A. Jones. Boston Book Co., Boston, Mass. Vol. I, 1770-1800, 1888; Vol. IV, 1800-1899, 1899.

KETTLEBOROUGH, CHARLES (compiled and edited by). *The State Constitutions and the Federal Constitution and Organic Laws of the Territories and Other Colonial Dependencies of the United States of America.* B. F. Bowen and Co., Indianapolis, Ind. 1918. pp. 1645.

Lawyers' Reports, Annotated. Lawyers' Coöperative Publishing Co., Rochester, N. Y.

Lawyers' Reports Annotated (New Series). Lawyers' Coöperative Publishing Co., Rochester, N. Y.

LISCHKA, CHARLES N. (Compiler). *Private Schools and State Laws.* Education Bulletin No. 4, National Catholic Welfare Conference Bureau of Education, Washington, D. C. 1924. pp. 220.

MEEK, CHARLES S. "The Relation of Religious Instruction to Public School Education." *National Education Association, Department of Superintendence Official Report.* Washington, D. C., 1926. pp. 195-99.

National Reporter System. Atlantic Reporter; Northeastern Reporter; North-Western Reporter; Southeastern Reporter; Pacific Reporter; Southern Reporter; Southwestern Reporter. West Publishing Co., St. Paul, Minn.

REISNER, EDWARD H. *Nationalism and Education Since 1789.* Macmillan Co., New York City, N. Y. 1923. pp. 575.

Ruling Case Law. Vol. XXIV. Edward Thompson Co., Northport, N. Y. Bancroft-Whitney Co., San Francisco, Cal. Lawyers' Coöperative Publishing Co., Rochester, N. Y.

Shepard's Citations of the Various States. (Published from time to time as cases are decided.) The Frank Shepard Co., New York City, N. Y.

State and Federal Reports. See the State Reporter Systems of the various states; and Reports of the United States Courts and of the District of Columbia.

Statutes at Large of the United States of America. Edited, printed and published by authority of Congress under the direction of the Secretary of State. Government Printing Office, Washington, D. C. Published as passed.

STRAYER, GEORGE D. "Legal Aspects of Moral Education." *Religious Education,* Vol. V, No. 6, Feb., 1911. pp. 599-611.

TIFFANY, ORRIN E. "State Laws Relative to Use of the Bible in or by the Public Schools." *Religious Education,* Vol. XXI, No. 1, 76-80. Feb., 1926.

TRUSLER, HARRY R. "The Authority of the Teacher." *American School Board Journal,* Vol. 54: 29-31, 60. Jan., 1917.

TRUSLER, HARRY R. "Compulsory Sex Hygiene and Examination." *American Law Review,* Vol. 55: 233-250. May, 1921.

TRUSLER, HARRY R. "Contractual Capacity and Liability of Public Schools."

American School Board Journal, Vol. 51: 14-15, 66. Oct., 1915; 15-16, 67. Nov., 1915.

TRUSLER, HARRY R. "Illegal Expenditures of School Money." *American School Board Journal,* Vol. 50: 19-20, 78. Feb., 1915.

TRUSLER, HARRY R. "Law and Its Relation to Schools and Teachers." *American School Board Journal,* Vol. 65: 53, 139. Sept., 1922.

TRUSLER, HARRY R. "Legal and Illegal Uses of School Buildings." *American School Board Journal,* Vol. 47: 9-10, 63. Nov., 1913.

TRUSLER, HARRY R. "Legality of Incidental Fees of Public Schools." *American School Board Journal,* Vol. 50: 17-18, 74. May, 1915.

TRUSLER, HARRY R. "Legal Rights of Excluded Pupils." *American School Board Journal,* Vol. 54: 16, 81. May, 1917; 18, 85. June, 1917.

TRUSLER, HARRY R. "Private Schools and the Law." *American School Board Journal.* Vol. 60: 42, 119. May, 1920.

TRUSLER, HARRY R. "Privileges and Liabilities of Pupils." *American School Board Journal.* Vol. 55: 23-24, 46. Oct., 1917.

TRUSLER, HARRY R. "Recent Decisions of School Law." *American School Board Journal.* Vol. 69: 37-38, 147, Aug., 1924; 39-41, Sept., 1924.

TRUSLER, HARRY R. "Rights of Pupils in Public Schools." *American School Board Journal,* Vol. 53: 28-29, 66, Nov., 1916; 29, 68, Dec., 1916.

TRUSLER, HARRY R. "The School and the Liberty of the Citizen." *American School Board Journal,* Vol. 65: 41-43, Oct., 1922.

TRUSLER, HARRY R. "Should the City Absorb the School." *American School Board Journal,* Vol. 50: 16, July, 1915.

TRUSLER, HARRY R. "State High School Athletic Associations." *American School Board Journal,* Vol. 70: 40, June, 1925.

TRUSLER, HARRY R. "The Status and Regulations of Private Schools." *American School Board Journal,* Vol. 59: 41, 99, Dec., 1919; Vol. 60: 32-44, 103, Jan., 1920.

VOORHEES, HARVEY C. *The Law of the Public School Systems of the United States.* Little, Brown, and Co., Boston, Mass. 1916. pp. 429.

WEIGLE, LUTHER A. "The Secularization of Public Education." *Religious Education,* Vol. XXI, No. 1, 90-96. Feb., 1926.

Words and Phrases Judicially Defined. Collected, edited and compiled by members of the editorial staff of the National Reporter System. West Publishing Co., St. Paul, Minn. 1904. 8 Volumes.

Words and Phrases (Second Series). Collected, edited and compiled by members of the editorial staff of the National Reporter System. West Publishing Co., St. Paul, Minn. 1914. 4 Volumes.

ZOLLMANN, CARL. "Historical Background of Religious Day Schools." *Religious Education,* Chicago, Ill. Vol. XXI, No. 1, 80-90. Feb., 1926.